What is Jihad?

Afaf Mougou

What is Jihad?
Toward a theory of Jihad in Political Discourse

PETER LANG

Lausanne · Berlin · Bruxelles · Chennai · New York · Oxford

Library of Congress Cataloging-in-Publication Data
A CIP catalog record for this book has been applied for at the
Library of Congress.

**Bibliographic Information published by the
Deutsche Nationalbibliothek**
The Deutsche Nationalbibliothek lists this publication in the
Deutsche Nationalbibliografie; detailed bibliographic data is
available online at http://dnb.d-nb.de.

Cover illustration: Treasure Chest - Open Ancient Trunk With Glowing
Magic Lights In The Dark stock photo
© Copyright by RomoloTavani

ISBN 978-3-631-89683-9 (Print)
E-ISBN 978-3-631-89830-7 (E-PDF)
E-ISBN 978-3-631-89831-4 (EPUB)
DOI 10.3726/b20633

© 2023 Peter Lang Group AG, Lausanne
Published by:
Peter Lang GmbH, Berlin, Deutschland

info@peterlang.com - www.peterlang.com

To Jocelyne Cesari

Table of Contents

Preface

The non-prototypical meaning of jihad was carried through time, by powerful and self-conscious traditions of thought often sedimented institutionally and politically. *How* the semantic system or framework of *Jihad* is shaped, however, varies a good deal.

My concern in this book is not with Jihad as a tradition that has retained a remarkable vivacity and strength well into our own times, couched in a language that would be broadly familiar to those who largely created the "war against terrorism" or debating against it.

My concern, is rather, with Jihad as a theory that has been veiled and misunderstood, in comparison with the flowering of writing about the tradition of Jihad since the second century of hijrah (Khadduri, Majid. 1940). Indeed, I think that there is an increasing set of problems in the tradition of Jihad, problems that, although fed by many forks, are becoming more and more noticeable in the context of the events of 11 September 2001 and their aftereffects. It seems important at this time, therefore, to question the Qur'anic text about the theory of Jihad, and whether the tradition has resources in it. Finally, at the close of the book, I shall offer a thought on whether the gradual increase of Jihad as a tradition of war would be compatible with the theory of Jihad, or opposed to it.

The war meaning of Jihad, is mentioned, in Qur'an, as a non-prototypical meaning that is one among other competing meanings that determine the relationship between the believer and politics of his belief.

Jihad is shaped through the webs of meanings that are related both: to a sub-conceptual structures like *religion is a journey* or *religion is a commerce*, and a main-conceptual structure which is *religion is balance*.

And because no linguistic work has been done about Jihad as a theory, I have attempted to evaluate it in the broadest possible manner, including as much interpretation elaborated by the Tunisian exegetist Mohamed Taher Ibn Ashour as possible, without compromising the huge connections that the notion of Jihad might establish with other words of Qur'an.

In order to defend this view, I will analyze in *part one* the relationship between the original meaning of Jihad and the rich image of journey, and I will explain how Jihad is conceptually structured in Qur'an around two axes that will be dealt with in *part two*: in the first axis, Jihad is a component of a rich image projection onto religion frame, and in the second one, Jihad is a component of a schematic projection onto the same frame of religion.

In the current context, this means that I suggest a new reading of Islamic holy books; Qur'an and the Bible, which can be united in one book that I call the "Qur'Bible" Text, and this union is based on the common conceptual structure that I have discovered in both texts the Qur'an and the Bible. This new reading goes beyond the literal meaning of religious texts, toward a conceptual global meaning that is based on the blending theory.

Hence, focus will be put on the concept of Jihad in Qur'an, a concept, once discovered, could, in my opinion, offer a solid ground on which both just war and Jihad traditions could be reviewed and reevaluated.

Jihad, as a practice that began from the revelation period until nowadays, has to exist in tension with the dominant political and ethical traditions of modern societies that are, in essence, hostile to it. In fact, the essential goal of modern societies, is peace that can guarantee freedom, the essential threat to this freedom is the uncontrolled power which, we can all agree, can be found more often either in the "uncovered" war situations, or in the context of a "covered" war that could grow outside a straight forward tyranny. The Jihad as a terrorist practice, however, is echoing a certain understanding of the relationship between war and politics that has the opposition to cultural injustice, as its central assumption, and assumes as a result that there may be circumstances where not only war is preferable to peace, but rather, "hidden" or "covered" war is preferable to declared one, if peace would amount to a surrender to injustice. *Part three* will give an analysis of the conceptual blending operations that lay behind this injustice.

The linguistic perspective of my work, is to show that blended spaces are not merely conceptual structures realized linguistically, but, that they are, as well, essential to the characterization of relevance. I want to argue that conceptual integration process is a necessary condition for relevance. As a discourse proceeds, the hearer constructs and then processes a number of assumptions. These form a gradually changing background against which new blended roles are processed, and this blending process involves strengthening contextual effects of these assumptions in the hearer's mind, which is a necessary condition for relevance, because the greater the contextual effects, the greater the relevance.

I consider my research within a larger framework of two linguistic approaches: Blending theory (Fauconnier and Turner. 2002), and the theory of Relevance (Sperber and Wilson. 1986).

In the first theory, Fauconnier and Turner, suggested a cognitive approach to language based on addressing the structural patterns exhibited by blended spaces. This approach centered itself within the study of operations that are behind the production of blended spaces in **language**. But their relation to the notion of relevance remained limited. Thus, blending theory has insufficiently considered the global integrated conceptual system which involves linguistic communicative functions.

The second theory was concerned with processes by which assumptions can be relevant, and based the notion of relevance on the value of the psychological models which make use of it, and, in particular, on the value of the theory of verbal comprehension that was formulated by Sperber and Wilson. But this enterprise has generally not addressed the tight relation it might be between relevance and blended spaces.

I see both theories as suggestive and complementary, but we do not regard them as conclusive. They will provide me with a starting point, *but are* certainly not to be treated as unique and final criterion.

This cognitive perspective of communication, goes further to inform most of my aim in this research, in fact, my research here is about "Jihad" as a conceptual structure, hence, it would address the interrelationships of conceptual structures, such as those in blended spaces, metaphoric mapping, semantic frame, conceptual categories, in order to group them into a large structuring system governed by a new model of communication that I seek to ascertain. This new model goes beyond the code and inferential models, toward the elaboration of what we might call "the categorial model" of communication, which would be inspired from the Blending theory.

The term "categorial", here, refers to the notion of "conceptual category" which is, contrary to the traditional view of formal semantics, an "embodied structure" that does not exist objectively "in the world" separated from human existence, but, it is, rather, correlated with our bodily experience; our minds, our biological life, and our imaginative capacities. The relatively recent tradition of cognitive linguistics has centered itself within the important role of imagination in the construal of categories, and this is proved by the prominent use of metaphors and metonymies in our everyday language, hence, in our conceptual system which is basically metaphorical. (Lakoff and Johnson. 1980)

My research is adopting a cognitive perspective which is based on the assumption that "language faculty" is a reflection or a "specialization", of general-purpose cognitive abilities, and is governed by general neural processes; in fact I believe that there is a continuum between body-based cognition, but also cognition acquired on the basis of social and cultural experience, and language.

I think there is little ground for claiming that language, let alone syntax, is a separate "module" in the mind or in the brain, as it is adapted by Chomsky's cognitivism.

Instead, imagination is one of the major general cognitive abilities, and it is, in more technical terms, the ability to project concepts onto other concepts through imaginative devices as metaphor and metonymy.

The main purpose of this book is to (re)consider the communicative aspect of the concept of Jihad with respect to the meaning extension patterns recognized by cognitive linguistics (Lakoff1987; Lakoff and Johnson1980; Johnson1987; Fauconnier1984; Fauconnier and Turner. 2002). More specifically, I would like to argue:

First, that language is powerful, and the power of language comes from blending operations that are basic, mysterious, powerful, complex, mostly unconcious, and are at the heart of even the simplest possible meaning.

Words in both religious and political discourse prompt for mental spaces that are blended in a mental web in highly creative ways.

Second, That conceptual structure of Jihad plays a crucial role in communication. And for that purpose, I will rely on two kinds of interpretation; the first is represented by the Tunisian exegetist Muhammad al-Tahir ibn Ashur who presents in his exegesis, a modern Tunisian interpretation of Qur'ăn, that relates it to other holy books, and monotheistic religions. The second kind of interpretation is represented by Tunisians and their different ways of understanding . I am interested as well by the comparative perspective between Tunisian interpretation and kinds of interpretations that Americans assign to those words in different religious contexts. With respect to the American culture, perhaps in the long run, the interaction of different frames of religion will account for new findings about the conceptual integration functioning in communication process. Even then, though, frame differences will still be related to the same conceptual structures that stand behind the mind's hidden complexities, which is needed to ensure that conceptual similarities, is, in fact addressing what is known to be subjectively present in the mind.

Chapter 1 The relation of the original meaning of Jihad with the rich image of journey

All utterances where Jihad is mentioned in Qur'an (concordance book of Qur'an. pp.182–183), show two major meanings of Jihad: the first, is the literal meaning, the second is the contextual meaning. And, while the first one represents the original meaning that relates Jihad with the frame of journey, the second one is the cultural meaning that relates Jihad with the tradition of war.

And, here are the verses realizing both kinds of meanings: each verse will be followed by my own translation to its explanation as cited in the Arabic book التحرير والتنوير "Liberation and enlightnment" by the exegetist Muhammad al-Tahir ibn Ashur

1. Verses where the original meaning of Jihad, is more salient

The original meaning of Jihad is related to the frame of journey; literally "Jihad means making very big effort to walk in the way leading to one's target, and the translation of this term into English, may reflect the same meaning: "to strive is to try very hard to do or get something: to strive for perfection". In the following verses, Qur'an uses the term "jihad" in its original meaning, and this use, as we will notice, evokes other terms related to journey, such as "way", "right", and guidance.

53. And those who believe will say: "Are these the men who swore their strongest oaths by Allah, that they were with you?" All that they do will be in vain, and they will fall into (nothing but) ruin. (Maida).

The expression "strongest oaths" is expressed in Arabic by a term derived from the same root of Jihad, which is "Jahd" "جهد أيمانهم", and we find in the explanation that Ibn Achour provides for this term, a tight relation with the travel frame: "the "jahd" of oaths is the strongest and firmest ones, and "jahd" in its literal meaning, is tiredness and hardship and the **extreme energy** (..) and I have never noticed such a use of the word "jahd" before Qur'an." (Liberation and Enlightenment. التحرير و التنوير Vol.4. p. 233.).

19. Do ye make the giving of drink to pilgrims, or the maintenance of the Sacred Mosque, equal to [the pious service of] those who believe in Allah and the Last Day, and strive with might and main in the way of Allah? They are not comparable in the sight of Allah: and Allah guides not those who do wrong(Tauba).

6. And if any strive [with might and main], they do so for their own souls: for Allah is free of all needs from all creation. The Spider.

Jihad is the exaggeration in making effort and is derived from the verb Jahada (جهد), and means perseverance with working and fatigue in doing hard work, for that reason it is current to use it for fighting in supporting Islam, and probably that what is meant by "Jihad" in this verse, is to bear patiently difficulties and harm that Muslims have been afflicted with because they believed in Islam and discarded polytheism, since they were harmed by pagan (..) thus, the use of Jihad here, is the same as its use in the prophet declaration: "We came back from the Junior Jihad to the Major Jihad". And this is the occurring meaning in this Surat, because it is revealed in Mecca where Jihad did not mean fighting. And the sense of "they do so for their own souls" is that all hardship that the Mujahid encounters, it is for his advantage because it supplies him with firmness in faith with which he will be saved from punishment in the afterlife. (Liberation and enlightenment. التحرير والتنوير Vol.10. p. 210.).

8. We have enjoined on man kindness to parents: but if they [either of them] strive [to force] thee to join with Me [in worship] anything of which thou hast no knowledge, obey them not. Ye have [all] to return to me, and I will tell you[the truth] of all that ye did. (The Spider).

"Striving is going too far in making effort at work, and what is meant here, is: if your parents insist that you become a polytheist."(Liberation and enlightenment. التحرير والتنوير Vol.10. p.214.)

15. "But if they _strive_ to make thee join in worship with Me things of which thou hast no knowledge, obey them not; yet _bear_ them _company_ in this life with _justice_ [and consideration], and _follow_ the way of those who _turn_ to me [in love]: in the _end_ the _return_ of you all is to Me, and I will tell you the _truth_ [and meaning] of all that ye did."(Luqman).

(..)and the striving is walking very hard and insistently, and the intended meaning is: if they insist in calling you to polytheism, then do not obey them. (..) and what is intended by "following the way of those who turn to God", is following the example of those who turned to God, that is those who repented their disbelief, and we have previously explained the "return" to God (الإنابة) in Surat Rum when he said "turning to him" and in Surat Hud, thus, it is intended by "who turn to me" those who abandoned polytheism and all that is forbidden like disobeying parents who are calling for monotheism (Liberation and enlightenment. التحرير والتنوير Vol.10. pp. 160–161.).

142. Did ye think that ye would enter Heaven without Allah testing those of you who fought hard [In His Cause] and remained steadfast?. (Al-i-imran).

Jihad evokes patience, because patience is the cause of success in Jihad (Liberation and Enlightenment. التحرير والتنوير Vol.3. p. 106).

72. Those who believed, and adopted exile, and strive for the Faith, with their property and their persons, in the *way* of Allah, as well as those who gave[them] asylum and aid, – these are [all] friends and protectors, one of another. (Anfal).

Ibn Achour explains "striving" (Jihad) here, as almost a synonym of Exodus (the Hegira): "This verse mentioned scales of people who embraced Islam, and started by showing two groups that were unified in guardianship (Wilaya ولاية) which are the emigrants and "Ansar" (people who helped them) who were privileged by supporting the religion. In fact, emigrants were privileged by preceding to support Islam and to bear leaving their homeland. And "Ansar" were privileged by lodging them, and on this basis it was shown that they are innocent from polytheism and its folks, and both groups shared the fact that they believed and that they strived (..) And the "Hegira" is quitting ones homeland, and going out of it, and leaving it (..) The origin of the word "Hegira" is leaving, and in particular, leaving ones home and people (..)And "Hegira" (exodus) was the most famous case of those who were opposed to their people, Ibrahim -Peace be on him- has emigrated and said: "I am going to my God who will show me his way", and so did Lot -Peace be on him- and said: "I am emigrating to my God the dearest and wisest", and so did Moses -Peace be on him- who emigrated with his people, and so did Mohammad -Peace be with him- and Muslims emigrated at his orders to El Habacha, and then to Medina Yathrib" (Liberation and Enlightenment. التحرير والتنوير Vol.6. pp. 83–84).

69. And those who *strive* in Our [cause],- We will certainly *guide* them to our *Paths*: For verily Allah is with those who do *right*. (Spider).

those whom *strove* in God are the early believers, and this striving is having patience with trouble and harm, and pushing the enemy cunning. (..) and meaning of "strive in our cause" is striving for the sake of God, and for the religion that he chose for the believers.(..) and the *"guidance"* is: directing (or showing the way), success thanks to heart facilitation and religious leading. And *God's paths* are deeds leading to his satisfaction and reward, they are compared to the ways taking to the generous man's house, the man who welcomes his guest. And what is meant by *"who do right"* all those who were right, that is to say, who took "right deeds" as a slogan, and this term implies praising believers and considering them as the previous prophets and reformists. (Liberation and enlightenment. التحرير والتنوير Vol.10. pp.36–37.)

9. O Prophet! *Strive hard* against the Unbelievers and the Hypocrites, and be firm against them. Their abode is Hell, – an evil refuge [indeed](Tahrim).

It is possible that the verb (جاهد) is used in the literal and metaphorical meaning, which are Jihad by weapon and Jihad by giving the proof and showing to the hypocrite his hypocrisy, this is called, metaphorically, "jihad", as it is shown in the prophet utterance: "we came back from the junior Jihad to the major one.", as well as in his reply to whom asked him to strive: "do you have parents? The man said: yes, he said: in them, you should strive(ففيهما فجاهد). (Liberation and enlightenment. التحرير والتنوير Vol.13. p. 372.)

In the explanation of Ibn Ashour, we notice that the tradition of Jihad as war, became so strong, that it took the place of the literal meaning of jihad.

52. Therefore listen not to the Unbelievers, but strive against them herewith with a great endeavour (وجاهدهم به جهادا كبيرا). (Furqan).

After he(God) warned him (the prophet) from losing power in appealing to Islam, he ordered him to be devoted to this matter, and he expressed this idea in terms of Jihad, which is the generic term for the extreme energy, and the verb mode (جاهد/فاعَلَ)implies contrasting their (disbelievers) effort with his effort that must not weaken and become feeble, and for that it is described the major Jihad (الجهاد الأكبر), namely inclusive of all kinds of Jihad (الجامع لكل مجاهدة).(Liberation and enlightenment. Vol.9. p. 53.)

1. O ye who believe! Take not my enemies and yours as friends [or protectors], -offering them [your] love, even though they have rejected the Truth that has come to you, and have [on the contrary] driven out the Prophet and yourselves[from your homes], [simply] because ye believe in Allah your Lord! If ye have come out *to strive in My Way* and to seek My Good Pleasure, [take them not as friends], holding secret converse of love [and friendship] with them: for I know full well all that ye conceal and all that ye reveal. And any of you that does this has *strayed from the Straight Path*. (Mumtahana).

2. Verses where the contextual meaning of Jihad, is more salient

218. Those who believed and those who suffered exile and fought [and strove and struggled] in the path of Allah, – they have the hope of the Mercy of Allah: And Allah is Oft-forgiving, Most Merciful. (Baqara).

This is the first occurrence of the term "Jihad" in Qur`an, Ibn Achour explains the meaning of it, as "(…) derived from the effort which is the hardship, because it involves adding one's effort to the effort of someone else to support the religion"(Liberation and Enlightenment. التحريروالتنوير Vol.2, p. 337).

41. Go ye forth, [whether equipped] lightly or heavily, and strive and struggle, with your goods and your persons, in the way of Allah. That is best for you, if ye [but] knew. (Tauba).

What is meant here, is going for Jihad (..) and "lightly" is an adverb derived from lightness, which is a state of the body implying the fewness of the quantity of its parts in comparison with other known bodies, and thus, it would be easy to move or carry it, which is the contrary of "heavily", (..)lightness and heaviness are, here, metaphors for the like states of the army; in fact, lightness is a metaphor for quickness in war, and it was a good sign of courage and aid, while heaviness matches with endurance in fighting (..) and striving is battling against the enemy, and it is derived from "Johd" (effort)- which means giving ones capacity in battling, and it denotes _defense by weapons_ (المدافعة بالسلاح) and thus, its use to mean spending money in invasion through expending money on troops and buying weapons, is a metaphorical use. (Liberation and enlightment. التحرير والتنوير Vol.6. pp. 206–207).

38. O ye who believe! what is the matter with you, that, when ye are asked to go forth in the *way* of Allah, ye cling heavily to the earth? Do ye prefer the life of this world to the Hereafter? But little is the comfort of this life, as compared with the Hereafter.(Tauba).

This discourse is addressed to believers for incitement to striving for God's way, and it is said in the manner of a blame on their retardation to respond to the alert for Jihad, and what is intended here, is Tabuk invasion (غزوة تبوك). Ibn Attia said: "There is no disagreement between scientists this verse was revealed as a blame to whom were absent in Tabuk invasion, in fact, many tribes and men among believers and hypocrites, were absent from this invasion" (Liberation and enlightenment. Vol.6. pp. 195–196).

110. But verily thy Lord, – to those who leave their homes after trials and persecutions, – and who thereafter strive and fight for the faith and patiently persevere, – Thy Lord, after all this is oft-forgiving, Most Merciful. (Nahl).

Striving is resistance using ones effort, that is ones energy (المجاهدة: المقاومة بالجهد، أي الطاقة).What is meant by "striving" here, is their self- defense against polytheists (Muchrikin المشركين) from giving them back to disbelief (Liberation and enlightenment. Vol.7. p. 300).

This verse was revealed in Makkah, before the start of Jihad as fighting disbelievers for religion support, which means that Jihad, in its beginning, didn't have the meaning of fighting.

9. O Prophet! *Strive hard* against the Unbelievers and the Hypocrites, and be firm against them. Their abode is Hell, – an evil refuge [indeed].(Tahrim).

It is possible that the verb (جاهد) is used in the literal and metaphorical meaning, which are Jihad by weapon and Jihad by giving the proof and showing to the hypocrite his hypocrisy, this is called, metaphorically, "jihad", as it is shown in the prophet utterance: "we came back from the junior Jihad to the major one.", as well as in his reply to whom asked him to strive: "do you have parents? The man said: yes, he said: in them, you should strive(ففيهما فجاهد). (Liberation and enlightenment. Vol.13. p.372)

In the explanation of Ibn Ashour, we notice that the tradition of Jihad as war, became so strong, that it took the place of the literal meaning of jihad.

78. *And strive in His cause the true striving,* (وجاهدوا في الله حقّ جهاده) [with sincerity and under discipline]. He has chosen you, and has imposed no difficulties on you in religion; it is the cult of your father Abraham. It is He Who has named you Muslims, both before and in this [Revelation]; that the Messenger may be a witness for you, and ye be witnesses for mankind! So establish regular Prayer, give regular Charity, and hold fast to Allah! He is your Protector – the Best to protect and the Best to help! (Hajj).

Jihad is a tradition in fighting Muslim's enemies for raising the word of Islam and defending it, The prophet explained it by saying: "who fights for the word of Allah to be the highest one, then, he is in God's way". And it is cited that the prophet - may God give him thanks and peace- when he came back from Tabuk invasion, said to his companions: "We have returned from the junior Jihad to the major Jihad", and he explained that it is the striving of the human being against his fancy, and it is used metaphorically to call the self-interdiction from committing sins, Jihad. (..) and "the true Jihad" means the pure one, that is to say Jihad not corrupted by default, and this verse is an order to Jihad, and maybe it is the first verse mentioned as an order to Jihad because part of this Surah was revealed in Mecca and the other part in Medina. (Liberation and enlightenment. التحرير والتنوير Vol.8. pp. 347–348)

95. Not equal are those believers who sit [at home] and receive no hurt, and those who strive and fight in the *way* of Allah with their goods and their persons. Allah hath granted a grade higher to those who strive and fight with their goods and persons than to those who sit [at home]. Unto all [in Faith]Hath Allah promised good: But those who strive and fight Hath He distinguished above those who sit [at home] by a special reward. (Nisaa).

This verse of surah of Nisaa is related to a previous verse where God was blaming some wrong practices of Muslims that kill others wrongly on name of Jihad:

94. O ye who believe! When ye go abroad in the *way* of Allah, investigate carefully, and say not to anyone who offers you a salutation: "Thou art none of a believer!" Coveting the perishable goods of this life: with Allah are profits and spoils abundant. Even thus were ye yourselves before, till Allah conferred on you His favors: Therefore carefully investigate. For Allah is well aware of all that ye do.

Ibn Achour explains this verse by relating it with the contextual effects that it evokes; he says: "(...) this verse is addressed to believers to warn them against killing other believers unfairly, and this verse was reveled in a particular case that

Boukhari transmitted from Ibn Abbes, he said: there was a man who had a small sheep, and Muslims caught up with him . He said: may peace be on you, but they killed him and took his sheep, that's why God has revealed this verse."(Liberation and Enlightenment. التحرير والتنوير Vol.3. p.166).

Chapter 2 The conceptual network of Jihad

1. Frames of religion and journey

1.1. The frame of religion in Qur'an

The frame is the system in which concepts are so interrelated that you cannot understand one concept unless you understand the whole structure. And if you mention one element included in a specific structure, in a text or conversation, then, this element call, automatically, for the other element of the frame. (Fillmore.1982. p.111).

The frame of religion in Qur'an can be presented by the following schema:

religion(Polytheism(value(disbelief),(Judaism(value(faith/disbelief)))),
Christianism(Islam(value(faith/disbelief))))(Islam(value(faith)))
Space:(God(value(one)))(God-Jusus-Mary(value(many)))(idols(vale(many)))
    (two Gods(value(many)))
Space: (satan(value(evil)))
Space: (good (value(true)))
Space: (evil(value(untrue)))
Space:(Muslims(value(believers)))(peopleofthescripture(believers/disbelievers)))
    (polytheists(value(disbelievers)))(sabaeans (value(disbelievers)))(magians(val
    ue(disbelievers)))
Space:(message(value(Qur'an/Torah/ New testament)))
Space: (messanger(value(Muhammed/Moses/Jesus)))
Space: (deeds(value(good/evil)))
Space: (Jihad(value(faith protection)))
Space: (reward(value(delight))) (punishment(value(hell)))

Religion's frame in Qur'an, has been culturally enriched with changes in societies over time, since the time of revelation. In fact, modern Muslim understanding of religion, is not the same as it is used to be for early Muslims. The meaning assigned to the previous elements of the frame, is in perpetual change in accordance with the evolution of religion frame. Thus, new values may be activated and get stronger than others, such as : reward, punishment, striving, praying, Satan,(…) while the activation of other values that were strong in the old frames, may become weak nowadays, such as : idols, ascribing partners (unto God), angels, trade, way,(…) Religion frame represents the conceptual background on the ground of which, the religious meaning of striving, in fact, striving cannot be meaningful unless it is related to other frame components like : God, message, disbelief (..), and the use of a single word among those ones, will activate in our minds, the whole structure of the frame.

Nowadays, we notice that the meaning assigned to Jihad (specifically in "Jihadist" operations) is identified by the activation of the concept of "terrorism" which is an element that was not entailed by Qur'anic religion frame. In fact, this new element is rather related to political orientations, and conflict between ideologies, which has yielded an essential change in Muslim mind, and has imposed a new distribution of religious force toward a salience of "Jihad"- terrorism, as a prototypical element in understanding Jihad. The prominent role of prototypical elements was pointed out by Fillmore who insisted on a crucial point in his frame semantics: "the determination of frames components inside a society, must be on the basis of cultural prototypes expanded in that society (Fillmore. 1982. pp. 117–118).

1.2. The frame of journey

Our transportation activity is usually conceptualized through basic concepts like journey, which is subdivided into subcategories such as journey by land, sea and air.

Transportation	Superordinate level
Journey-excursion-promenade..	Basic level
Journey by land, sea, air…	Infraordinatelevel

The frame of journey is a rich image composed by a set of elements that can be developed and enriched according to the experience.

Frame: journey(category(value(movement in space and time)))

Subframe1: (departure(value(start))):
Space(journeyer(value(moving away)))
Space(target(value(studying, teaching, tourism, pilgrimage to Mecca..)))
Space(preparedness(value(*provision*)))
Space(*migration*(value(leaving one's home)))

Subframe2: (path(value(movement))):
Space(*way*(value(*straight/oblique*)))
Space(distance(value(traversing)))
Space(means of transport(value(*walking*/ She-camel/car/plane/boat…)))

Space(*hardship*(value(faraway destination/ storms/ robbers/ aggressors/ car damage/ load))))
Space(help(value(*guidance*)))
Space(*Jihad*(value(perseveration)))

Subframe3: (arrival(value(end))):
Space (reaching the purpose(value(*finding the right way*)))
Space (missing the purpose(value(*losing one's way/drift..*)))

Subframe4: (*returning*(value(going back to the starting point)))
We have underlined the chosen elements that were projected onto the frame of religion, and Jihad is one of those elements that we will mention their occurrences in Qur'an later on.

2. The blending operation and its realizations

2.1. Religion is a journey: The nest of Jihad

We argue here that Jihad is a component of a rich image projection. In fact, utterances in Qur'an, are produced by the blending process based on metaphorical projection between mental spaces (or domains). A blended space is a mental construal produced by the process of structuring an abstract concept through a concrete concept. Religion is an abstract concept that's why it is not clear in our minds and needs to be structured by concrete concepts like vision, trade, journey, and so on (Mougou. Conceptual metaphors in Qur'an.2014).

Concept of Jihad is a part of religion frame, and we want to show here how our conceptualization of Jihad is constructed through our conceptualization of the journey. In fact, the religious meaning of Jihad, as we have seen above, is the effort made by believers to reach God's satisfaction and protect their faith, and this abstract idea is clarified by "Jihad" which is an element brought from the journey's frame and connected to a larger lexical network widespread in Qur'an.

In our opinion, we cannot cover the theoretical basis of Jihad, unless we analyze the hidden blending process that does exist behind the use of this term in Qur'an.

For an explanation of this process, let's take the example of this verse:

That ye believe in Allah and His Messenger, and that ye strive [your utmost]in the Way of Allah.(Saff 61/11)

This utterance evokes the blending operation represented in (1):

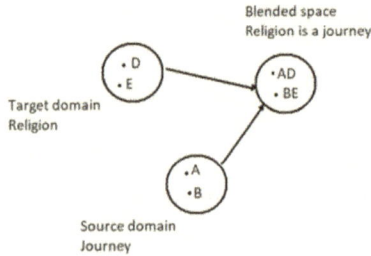

Blended space
Religion is a journey

Target domain
Religion

Source domain
Journey

(1)

The blending process in this verse, is based on the following stages:

- A{strive}, and B{way} are two roles belonging to the journey space which is the source domain.
- D{protection of one's belief}, and E{faith} are two values corresponding to A and B, and prompting for a target domain which is religion space.
- The Qur'anic context prompts for the projection of A and B onto D and E.
- The creation of a blended space (a new space) in which A (role1) is integrated with D(value1), and B (role2) is integrated with E (value2).
- The creation of two new blended roles: AD {the protection of one's belief is striving}, and BE {faith is a way}.

The expression "way of Allah" may seem irrelevant since it is based on the combination of two incompatible terms way(concrete)/ Allah(abstract). But the expression becomes acceptable and relevant inside the blend. The conceptual metaphor *religion is a journey* is the result of the combination between two different concepts (religion/journey), and this conceptual integration prompts for a linguistic combination realized in "way" and "strive" and a huge number of items spread in Qur'anic text and realizing the same conceptual structure. Some of them will be mentioned later on.

The blend is not a mere addition between different meanings of words, meanings provided by words seem, rather, very little in comparison with meanings that words prompt for. Thus, the blending process between roles belonging to different conceptual domains, seem to be a very creative process. (Fauconnier and Turner.2002)

The conceptual structure *religion is a journey* is based on the investment of most of journey frame elements by projecting them onto religion frame. As a result of this projection, a huge number of terms realizing *religion is journey* was generated in Qur'an. In the following examples, is mentioned a number of those terms organized according to the journey subframes.

In the presentation of blended roles, we will use the term "Mujahid" as a synonym of the term "journeyer".

Subframe 1: departure.

Blended role 1:

The Mujahid is the first to lead the way and prepare himself to a long journey= The believer is the precursor in making many good deeds to prepare himself to God's reward.
This blended role is realized in terms like:

– First :

"Say: "Nay! But I am commanded to be the first of those who bow to Allah [in Islam], and be not thou of the company of those who join gods with Allah."Anam6/14.

"No partner hath He: this am I commanded, and I am the first of those who bow to His will." Anam6/163.

"Glory be to Thee! to Thee I turn in repentance, and I am the first to believe." Tauba9/143.

"And the first to lead the way of Muhajirin and Ansar" Tauba9/100.

Besides, the "first" in Qur'an, refers to God:

"We mete out death among you, and We are not to be outrun" (Waqia56/60).

– Provision :

Provision is blended with piety: "So make provision for yourselves, for the best provision is to ward off evil" (Bakara2/197).

Blended role 2:
The Mujahid quits his home = The believer switches from disbelief to belief.
This blended role is realized in one term frequently used in Qur'an:

– Emigration :

"And Lot believed him, and said: Lo! I am a *fugitive* unto my Lord." El `Ankabout29/26.
"Lo ! those who believe , and those who *emigrate* and strive in the way of Allah, these have hope of Allah's mercy" El Bakara2/218.
"So those who *fled* and were driven forth from their homes and suffered damage for My cause, and fought and slain" Al 'imran3/195.

"He who migrateth in the cause of Allah, finds in the earth a refuge, wide and spacious" (Nisaa4/100).

Subframe2: path.

Blended role3:

The Mujahid *keeps going* along the *way* leading to his destination and is in a *pace* to arrive = The believer keeps doing good deeds seeking God's pleasure, andis trying to do his best in avoiding evil.

The "way"- Sabil (سبيل) is usually mentioned associated with the verbs: to strive(Jahada), (Hajara), and to kill (Kaatala), which are considered conceptually synonyms. The occurrence of "striving" evoques, automatically, the way the believer-striver-journeyer is going in.

The term "Sabil" is the journey's element most used in Qur'an, it is mentioned 175 times, and is usually added to the term of Allah "sabil Allah" which means Jihad: "Sabil Allah is Jihad, which it is called so because it is like a way leading to God, thus to his satisfaction" (Liberation and enlightenment.التحرير والتنوير. Vol.10. p. 197)

"Go ye forth, [whether equipped] lightly or heavily, and strive and struggle,with your goods and your persons, in the **way** of Allah.")Tauba9/41(.

"and that ye strive [your utmost]in the **way** of Allah." Saff61/11."Fighting in the **way** of Allah".)Maida5/57).

"those who suffered exile and fought in the **path** of Allah". (Baqara2/218).

"Those who leave their homes in the **way** of Allah" (Hajj22/58).

"He who forsakes his home in the **way** of Allah" (Nisaa4/100).

" Think not of those who are slain in Allah's **way** as dead. Nay, they live, finding their sustenance in the presence of their Lord" (Al-i-Imran3/190).

"Fight in the **way** of Allah those who fight you" (Baqara2/190).

"Verily this is an Admonition: therefore, whoso will, let him take a[straight] path to his Lord!" (Muzzammil73/17).

"in his saying "to his Lord" a comparison between the state of who is seeking gain and guidance and the state of the walker to a supporter or a noble person, who has been oriented to the way that leads him to his destination" (Liberation and enlightenment. التحرير والتنوير.Vol.29. p.278).

In some cases, "Sabil" is employed in a negative connotation and is usually associated with the adjective "crooked", or the noun "idol" and "unrighteous": Say: "O ye People of the Book! Why obstruct ye those who believe, from the path of Allah, Seeking to make it crooked" (Al-i-Imran).

"Those who love the life of this world more than the Hereafter, who hinder [men] from the Path of Allah and seek therein something crooked: they are astray by a long distance."(Ibraham14/3)."

"Those who believe do battle for the way of Allah, and those who disbelieve do battle for the way of idols"(Niss4/76).

"Thus do We expound the revelations that the way of the unrighteous may be manifest."(Anam6/55).

- "Sirat"

It is mentioned 45 times in Qur'an to mean "the right religion", and it is usually characterized as "right": "Show us the straight way" Fatiha1/6:

> "the straight is the way that is not crooked or zigzagged, and the best of the ways is the one that is straight because it is the nearest one to the destination, and the walkers cannot be lost or hesitated or annoyed" (Liberation and enlightenment. التحرير والتنوير. Vol.1.pp. 190–191).
> "Verily, this is My way, leading straight: follow it"(Anam.6/153).

- "Tarik"

The word "Tarik" is used 5 times to mean either Islam, like in: They said, "O our people! We have heard a Book revealed after Moses, confirming what came before it: it guides [men] to the Truth and to a Straight <u>Path</u>" Ahqaf46/30, or belief in God, like in: "There are among us some that are righteous, and some the contrary: we follow divergent paths"(Jinn72/11).

- Going before in a pace :

Words related to "pace" is used to refer to powers of goodness; God, God's word(Jesus), Qur'an, believers' good deeds.

> "We mete out death among you, and We are not to be <u>outrun</u>" (Waqia56/60).
> "Mankind was but one nation, but differed [later]. Had it not been for a word that <u>went forth before</u> from thy Lord, their differences would have been settled between them."(Yunus10/19).
> "We certainly gave the Book to Moses, but differences arose therein: had it not been that a word <u>had gone forth before</u> from thy Lord, the matter would have been decided between them, but they are in suspicious doubt concerning it."(Hud11/110).

> "Had it not been for an ordinance of Allah which <u>had gone before</u>, a severe penalty would have reached you for the [ransom] that ye took." (Anfal8/68).

> "And the <u>foremost</u> in the <u>race</u>, the <u>foremost</u> in the <u>race</u>" (Waqia56/10).

Blended role4:
The Mujahid is devoted to the way he is traversing = The believer surrenders to God's willing.

– "Islam"

Islam and all terms morphologically related to it, evoke the frame of journey, in fact, the believer who follows Qur'anic recommendations, is assimilated to the journeyer who follows God's way, which is a peaceful(laying down one's arm), safe and right(it leads to his target) way. And, the connection between "way" and peace, is clear in Qur'an: "Whereby Allah guideth him who seeketh His good pleasure unto paths of peace" (Maida5/16).

> Those who believe, those who are Jews, and the Sabaeans and the Christians, —any who believe in Allah and the Last Day, and work righteousness, —on them shall be no fear, nor shall they grieve. (Maida5/69)

> "Those who believe, and those who follow the Jewish[scriptures], and the Christians and the Sabians,- any who believe in Allah and the Last Day, and work righteousness, shall have their reward with their Lord; on them shall be no fear, nor shall they grieve". (Baqara2/62)

"If anyone desires a religion other than Islam [submission to Allah], never will it be accepted of him; and in the Hereafter He will be in the ranks of those who have lost [All spiritual good]". (Al-i-Imran3/85).

"The Religion before Allah is Islam [submission to His Will]" (Al-i-Imran3/19).

"Who can be better in religion than one who submits his whole self to Allah (أسلم وجهه لله), does good, and follows the way of Abraham the true in Faith. For Allah did take Abraham for a friend". (Nisaa4/125).

The assertion that religions like Judaism and Jews are accepted by God, in verses Maida69, and Baqara62, seem to be contradictory with verses in Al-i-Imran19, and Nisaa125, that likely, mention Islam as the religion of God. But, if we understand the terms "Islam"(إسلام) and "Aslama"(أسلم) in their original meaning, then, the contradiction will disappear.

In fact, Islam, literally, means: "to submit without resistance, not because you are powerless, but because you recognize the truth, and this appellation is more suitable, for this religion, than the one of "faith", because Islam is the most distinct aspect of *following* the prophet in the *truth* that he brought" (Liberation and enlightenment. التحرير والتنوير. Vol.3. p. 189).

Besides, the verb "Aslama" in the verse4/125, means: "submitting oneself to God's orders, thus, the extreme obedience, because "aslama" means to lay down one's arm and leave resistance" (Liberation and enlightenment. التحرير والتنوير. Vol.1.p. 674).

Both previous words, are derivate from the same root (س.ل.م), which relates them to other terms like (silm سلم) and (salam سلام): " 'Silm' is the contrary of war, and 'salam' is a synonym of it, in that it is the contrary of war, and the meaning of Islam's greeting, which is saying 'peace on you عليكم السلام', that is who addressed you the Islam's greeting, as a sign that he is muslim." (Liberation and enlightenment. التحرير والتنوير. Vol.3. p. 167).

Furthermore, it is sure that the tight conceptual relation between Islam and the peaceful way, is behind some translations to the words "Islam" and "aslama"(which are used in the Arabic- the language that Qur'an was revealed in, by "the surrender" and "to surrender":

> "Who is better in religion than he who surrendereth his purpose to Allah" (Nisaa4/125).
> "Lo! Religion with Allah (is) the Surrender (to His Will and Guidance)" (Al-i-Imran3/19).

Surrender (yourself to s.b) denotes in its literal meaning to stop fighting and admit that you have lost.

Blended role5:
The Mujahid is walking to his destination = The believer is holding fast to his faith.

This blended role is realized in the following items:

– "Walking"

This term is used to mean continuation of belief and understanding religion in order to be guided by it:

> "And the leader among them go away [impatiently], [saying], "Walk ye away, and remain constant to your gods!" (Sad38/6).
> "Can he who was dead, to whom We gave life, and a light whereby he can walk amongst men, be like him who is in the depths of darkness, from which he can never come out?"(Anam6/122).
> "He will provide for you a Light by which ye shall walk[straight in your path]." (Hadid57/28).

In his explanation to the latter verse, Ibn Ashour is dismounting elements that constitute the source domain scene: "His saying: "He will provide for you a Light by which ye shall walk" is a pattern of the state of folks who are looking for God's satisfaction as well as gaining felicity, and afraid that the contrary happens, after the state of folks *walking* in a *way* at *night* afraid of *being lost*, that are given a *light* to *guide* them and avoid *deviation* from the *right way*" (Liberation and enlightenment. التحرير والتنوير. Vol.27.p.429)

– "To hurry"

It is used in two contradictory meanings:

1/To make many good deeds:

> "They believe in Allah and the Last Day; they enjoin what is right, and forbid what is wrong; and they <u>hurry</u> in [all] good works: They are in the ranks of the righteous." (Al-i-Imran3/114).
> "<u>Hurry</u> up for forgiveness from your Lord"(Al-i-Imran3/133).
> "hurry in good work" is a pattern of the state of believers' initiative for good deeds, after the state of the walker who is rushing to reach his destination" (Liberation and enlightenment. التحرير والتنوير. Vol.4. p. 58.)

2/To make many bad deeds: "Let not their conduct grieve thee who <u>hurry</u> easily to disbelief"(Al-i-Imran3/176).

– "To flee"

This term is used in two contradictory meanings;

1/ Fleeing from wrong ways and following the right one, is:"quitting polytheism and giving up atheism, which is a comparison between their state of going astray and the state of the person who is in a scaring place calling himself to flee from it toward a saver" (Liberation and enlightenment. Vol.27.p.19): "Therefore flee unto Allah; Lol! I am a plain Warner unto you from Him"(Zarriat51/50).

2/To abandon Islam :"But my call only increases their flight from the Right". Nuh71/6).

Blended role6:

The Mujahid is following the steps of the right guide and must not be misled = The believer is applying God's orders and must not renounce from his religion.

– "Following"

It is blended either with the meaning of "extreme obedience to God": "and follow the light which is sent down with him"Araf 7/157, or with the opposed meaning of sin: "and follow not the footsteps of the devil"(Baqara2/168).

– "Guidance"

It is blended with the role of faith as in "And Allah doth advance in guidance those who seek guidance"(Maryam19/76).

– "To mislead"

It is blended with the meaning of making sins by imitating sinners: "Nor follow thou the lusts [of thy heart],for they will <u>mislead</u> thee from the Path of Allah: for those who wander astray"(Sad38/26).

– "Going wrong"

It is to make sins: "O ye who believe! Ye have charge of your own souls. He who go wrong cannot injure you if ye are rightly guided"(Maida5/105).

– "Turning back on one's heels/ turn back"

To renounce from Islam:

> "Muhammad is no more than a messenger: many were the messenger that passed away before him. If he died or were slain, will ye then <u>Turn back on your heels</u>?" (Al-i-Imran3/144).
> "If any <u>turn back</u> after this, they are perverted transgressors."(Al-i-Imran3/83).
> "Those who <u>turn back</u> as apostates after Guidance was clearly shown to them,-the Evil One has instigated them and busied them up with false hopes." (Muhammad47/25).

Blended role7:
The Mujahid encounters is helped by: signs, guides, refuges, his own power, powerful people, weapons, and companions (friends) = The believer is showed the right way by: Qur'an, prophets, the strength of his belief, God's power and protection, faithful people.

– "'Ayat'(verses)"

Verses (Ayat آيات in Arabic): "'Ayat' is the plural of 'Aya'(آية), and its linguistic original meaning is the sign guiding to the house or to the way" (Liberation and enlightenment. Vol. 1. pp. 463–464), which means in the blend, the proof leading to the truth. The term "Ayat" is very much widespread in Qur'an, here are some examples:

> "This because they went on rejecting the Signs of Allah and slaying His Messengers without just cause."(Baqara2/61).
> "We have sent down to thee Manifest Signs [ayat]; and none reject them but those who are perverse."(Baqara2/99).

– "To convey/' Balagh'"

Literally, "to convey" is "to take somebody/something from one place to another, especially in vehicle" which evokes journey's frame. Likewise, in Arabic "balagh

البلاغ" is "to take something to the destination" (Liberation and enlightenment. Vol.9.p.193).

In Qur'an, « Balagh/Iblagh إبلاغ » means the arrival of Islamic Law to those who are charged with, thus, Islamic Law is compared to the message that the journeyer (Mujahid) is conveying from a place to another, that's why the prophet is called « the messenger رسول » :

"I convey unto you the message of my Lord"(Araf7/62).
"but if they turn back, Thy duty is to convey the Message; and in Allah's sight are [all] His servants." (Al-i-Imran3/20).

- Refuge :

"The refuge" is used to refer to God who protects the believer and forgives him:
"…and they perceived that there is no refuge from Allah but to Himself. Then He turned to them, that they might repent: for Allah is the Relenting, Tthe Merciful." (Tauba9/118).
"Hearken ye to your Lord, before there come a Day which there will be no putting back, because of [the Ordainment of] Allah! that Day there will be for you no place of refuge nor will there be for you any room for denial [of your sins]!"(Shura42/47).

- Power :

"Power" in Qur'an, has 4 meanings:

1 Strength of belief: God calls believers to be aware of the right meaning of Qur'an and to be resolved in applying it:
"Hold strongly to what We have given you and bring [ever] to remembrance what is therein: Perchance ye may fear Allah."(Baqara2/63).

2 physical strength:

"And O my people! Ask forgiveness of your Lord, and turn to Him [in repentance]: He will send you the skies pouring abundant rain, and add power to your power: so turn ye not back in sin!" (Hud11/52).:
"their reward for having abandon polytheism is increasing their power by the increase of their number and the health of their bodies and abundance of their daily bread, because all this is a power for the nation, it makes her capable to manage without other nations and capable to be independent and makes other nations calling for her." (Liberation and enlightenment.Vol.6. pp. 96–97).

3 God's strength: "For Allah is He Who gives [all] Sustenance,- Lord of *Power*,- Steadfast [for ever]." (Zariyat51/58) .

4 The prophet's strength: "Verily this is the word of a most honorable Messenger, endued with *Power*, with rank before the Lord of the Throne" (Takwir81/20).

- Weapons/arms :

This term is not frequently used in Qur'an, it is mentioned only 4 times in the same verse, to refer to means of defense for believers:

> "When thou [O Messenger] art with them, and standest to lead them in prayer. Let one party of them stand up [in prayer] with thee, Taking their <u>arms</u> with them: When they finish their prostrations, let them Take their position in the rear. And let the other party come up which hath not yet prayed – and let them pray with thee, Taking all precaution, and bearing <u>arms</u>: the Unbelievers wish, if ye were negligent of your <u>arms</u> and your baggage, to assault you in a single rush. But there is no blame on you if ye put away your <u>arms</u> because of the inconvenience of rain or because ye are ill; but take [every] precaution for yourselves. For the Unbelievers Allah hath prepared a humiliating punishment."(Nisaa4/102).

The companions of the Mujahid are expressed in Qur'an either by the terms "guardians/ friends/ helpers, brothers (إخوان/أنصار/أصحاب / وليّ)", "walyy" in Arabic means "someone near <u>following</u> you" which refers to the journey frame. In the religious context, those terms refer to:

- Guardian/friend/helper (نصير)=God:

> "and ye have not, beside Allah, any <u>guardian</u> or helper?"(Baqara2/107).
> "Allah is the <u>Protector</u> of those who have faith: from the depths of darkness. He will lead them forth into light." (Baqara2/257).

> "Unto Allah belongeth the dominion of the heavens and the earth. He giveth life and He taketh it. Except for Him ye have no <u>protector</u> nor helper." (Tauba9/116).

> "Lo! Allah is an <u>enemy</u> to those who reject Faith."Baqara2/98.
> "But Allah hath full knowledge of your enemies: Allah is enough for a protector, and Allah is enough for a <u>Helper</u>."(Nisaa4/45).
> "Nay, Allah is your protector, and He is the best of <u>helpers</u>."(Al-i-Imran3/150).

- Friends/companions/brothers/helpers

(أنصار/ناصرين)=The community of believers :

> "The Believers, men and women, are <u>protectors</u> one of another: they enjoin what is just, and forbid what is evil." (Tauba9/71).

> "O ye who believe! Take not for <u>friends</u> unbelievers rather than believers: Do ye wish to offer Allah an open proof against yourselves?" (Nisaa4/144).

"But those who believe and work righteousness,- no burden do We place on any soul, but that which it can bear,- they will be <u>Companions of the Garden</u>"(Araf7/42).

The expression "companions of Garden" is very commonly used in Qur'an, as a counterpart of the expression "companions of fire" that we will see later on.

"When Jesus found Unbelief on their part He said: "Who will be My <u>helpers</u> to[the work of] Allah?" Said the disciples: "We are Allah's <u>helpers</u>: We believe in Allah, and do thou bear witness that we are Muslims." (Al-i-Imran3/52).
"Our Lord! any whom Thou dost admit to the Fire, Truly Thou coverest with shame, and never will wrong-doers Find any <u>helpers</u>!" (Al-i-Imran3/192).

- Friend=The prophet.

"Your <u>Companion</u> is neither astray nor being misled."(Najm53/2).
"And [O people!] your <u>companion</u> is not one possessed" (Takwir81/22).

Blended role8:
The Mujahid encounters hardship (Burden, charge, war, enemies) = The believer has difficulty in applying God's orders.

– "Burden"

The burden is the sin: "And removed from thee thy burden, the which did gall thy back?" (Acharh94/2).

– "charge"

The charge (الحمل) is "the carried luggage" (Liberation and enlightenment. Vol.20. pp. 220–221), and it is blended with the sense of God's commandment:

"Say: Obey Allah and obey the messenger. But if ye turn away, then (it is) for him (to do) only that wherewith he hath been charged, and for you (to do) only that wherewith ye have been charged" (Nur24/54).
"The similitude of those who were charged with the [obligations of the] Mosaic Law, but who subsequently failed in those [obligations], is that of a donkey which carries huge tomes" (Jumua62/5).

- War

In its literal meaning, the "war"(حرب), in Arabic, refers to the domain of "journey", ("حَرِبَ المسافر": أُخِذ جميعُ مالِه، و"وضعت الحربُ أوزارها (الوِزر: حِمل المسافر) (المعجم الوسيط)
the verb (حَرِبَ) refers to the journeyer who was stolen.

In English too, the word "war" is tightly related to the " journey" domain, as it evokes both meanings of "to carry" and move": "a conflict carried on by force of arms, as between nations or between parties within a nation; warfar, as by land, sea, or air.

late Old English *werre*, from an Anglo- Norman French variant of Old French *guerre*, from a Germanic base shared by worse.

The "Werre" is a_river in the Detmold region (Regierungsbezirk) of North Rhine-Westphalia, Germany, left tributary of the Weser. Its source is near Horn-Bad Meinberg. The Werre flows generally north through the towns Detmold, Lage, Bad Salzuflen, Herford and Löhne. It flows into the Weser close to Bad Oeynhausen. The total length of the Werre is 71.9 km. It crosses the districts of Lippe, Herford and Minden-Lübbecke.(Wiktionary).

In Hebrew, the word קְרָב, refers, in its original/literal meaning to "bitting each other while walking" which is related to path schema and fighting bodies along the path.

The word "war" in Qur'an, is a very weak role in the activation process of the blend. In fact, it is mentioned only 4 times:

1 "O you who believe! Observe your duty to Allah, and give up what remaineth (due to you) from usury, if you are (in truth) believers. And if you do not, then be warned of *war* (against you) from Allah and His messenger. And if you repent, then you have your principal (without interest). Wrong not, and you shall not be wronged. " (The cow2/ 278_279).

2 "As often as they light a fire for *war*, Allah extinguish it" (The Table5/65).

3 "If you come on them in the *war*, deal with them so as to strike fear in those who are behind them, that haply they may remember" (Spoils of war8/57).

4 "Now when you meet in battle those who disbelieve, then it is smiting of the necks until, when you have routed them, then making fast of bonds, and afterwards either grace or ransom till the *war* lay down its burdens" (Muhammad47/4).

– "enemy"

The Mujahid's enemies are:

• Satan

"O ye people! Eat of what is on earth, Lawful and good; and do not follow the footsteps of the evil one, for he is to you an avowed enemy."(Baqara2/168).

"Against them make ready your strength to the utmost of your power, including steeds of war, to strike terror into [the hearts of] the enemies of Allah and your enemies" (Anfal8/60).

"Said [the father]: "My [dear] little son! relate not thy vision to thy brothers, lest they concoct a plot against thee: for Satan is to man an avowed enemy!" (Yusuf5/12).

"Did I not enjoin on you, O ye Children of Adam, that ye should not worship Satan; for that he was to you an enemy avowed?-" (Ya-Sin36/60).

- Community of disbelievers :

"Those who believe fight in the way of Allah, and those who reject Faith Fight in the way of Evil: So fight ye against the friends of Satan: feeble indeed is the cunning of Satan." (Nisaa4/76) .
"Those who reject Faith,- neither their possessions nor their [numerous]
progeny will avail them aught against Allah: They will be companions of the Fire,- dwelling therein [for ever]"(Al-i-Imran3/116).
"When ye travel through the earth, there is no blame on you if ye shorten your prayers, for fear the Unbelievers May attack you: For the Unbelievers are unto you open enemies." (Nisaa4/101).

Blended role9:
The Mujahid strives to overcome the hardship = The believer struggles to protect his faith against aggressors.

- "Jihad"

As we have seen above, the original meaning of Jihad is the hard effort that the journeyer must make to keep going in the straightway leading to his destination. In the blended space, Jihad is the effort that the believer makes to obey God's commandment and protect his faith.

The occurrence of the term "Jihad" is very much spread in Qur'an:

"Or think ye that ye shall be abandoned, as though Allah did not know those among you who strive with might and main, and take none for friends and protectors except Allah, His Messenger, and the [community of] Believers? But Allah is well-acquainted with [all] that ye do." (Tauba9/16).
"And those who strive in Our Way,- We will certainly guide them to our Paths: For verily Allah is with those who do right." (Hujurat49/69).

"Were We then weary with the first Creation, that they should be in confused doubt about a new Creation? Hujurat49/15. "That ye believe in Allah and His Messenger, and that ye strive [your utmost] in the Cause of Allah, with your property and your persons: That will be best for you, if ye but knew! Saff61/11.

Subframe3: arrival(end of the journey).

Blended role10:
The Mujahid deviates from the right way and misses his destination and is led to a very dangerous place where there is fire= The believer renounces to Islam and is punished.

- "Fire/Hell"

The rich image of fire and hell "جهنم"is very much developed in Qur'an, and it is derived from the sub-conceptual metaphor *the non being is a place where there is fire*, which is related to the main metaphor *religion is a journey*. We can mention some of the verses where "fire" is mentioned :

> "But those who reject Faith and belie Our Signs, they shall be companions of the Fire; they shall abide therein."(Baqara2/39).

> "Thus will Allah show them [The fruits of] their deeds as [nothing but] regrets. Nor will there be a way for them out of the Fire."(Baqara2/167).

> "Say to those who reject Faith: "Soon will ye be vanquished and gathered together to Hell,-an evil bed indeed [to lie on]!"Al-i-(Imran3/12).

- « **Journey's end/** المصير»

The Arabic term of "Masir مصير" is translated into English by two terms that are evoking journey's frame:

> the first is "journey's end": "I shall leave him in contentment for a while, then i shall compel him to the doom of Fire-a hapless journey's end !" (Baqara2/126).
> the second is "destination" : "for a while will I grant them their pleasure, but will soon drive them to the torment of Fire,- an evil destination [indeed]!" (Baqara2/126).

In both cases, "Masir" is blended with the religious meaning of punishment.

- "Slide"

The slide (Zalla زلّة) in its literal meaning is "moving smoothly unintentionally one's foot", and it is blended with the meaning of "sin": "If yes slide back after the clear [Signs] have come to you, then know that Allah is Exalted in Power, Wise." (Baqara2/209).

"Deviation"

> He it is Who has sent down to thee the Book: In it are verses basic or fundamental [of established meaning]; they are the foundation of the Book: others are allegorical. But those in whose hearts is deviation follow the part there of that is allegorical, seeking

discord, and searching for its hidden meanings, but no one knows its hidden meanings
except Allah.(Al-i-Imran3/7).

- "Straying"

Straying (in Arabic Dhalal ضلال) is blended with the meaning of punishment: "Truly those in sin are the ones straying in mind, and mad." Qamar54/47.

- « Refuge/ملجأ »

In this context, the word "refuge" is used in the opposite sense it was used above,
in fact, in case the Mujahid's belief is weak, he will search a refuge to escape from
Allah, as it is in the following verse:

> If they could find a refuge, or caves, or a place of concealment, they would turn straight-
> away there to, with an obstinate rush. (Tauba9/57).

Subframe 4: returning.

Blended role11:
The Mujahid reaches his destination and returns to the start point = The believer
meets God and is rewarded.

- "Returning"

This journey's role is blended with "resurrection": "How can ye reject the faith in
Allah?- seeing that ye were without life, and He gave you life; then will He cause
you to die, and will again bring you to life; and again to Him will ye return."
(Baqara2/28).

> [To the righteous soul will be said:] "O [thou] soul, in [complete] rest and satisfac-
> tion! Come back thou to thy Lord,- well pleased [thyself], and well-pleasing unto Him!
> (Fajr89/27–28).

- "Abode"

Abode (in Arabic "Ma'ab"مآب) is "to return to the starting place (..) their resurrection and their bringing to Him, is compared to the return of the journeyer to
his abode" (Liberation and enlightenment. Vol.30. p. 308) : "Allah ! With Him is
a more excellent abode" (Al-i-Imran3/14).

- "journey's end"

> It is "the appearance of truths and the compliance of the servant with His God"
> (Liberation and enlightenment. Vol.25. p. 156) : "Allah is the Sovereignty of the heavens
> and the earth and all that is between them, and unto Him is the journeying" Maida5/18.

Blended role13:
The Mujahid is in "Gardens underneath which rivers flow" = The believer is in the eternity.

This blended role is based on the sub-conceptual metaphor *eternity is a garden* which is related to the main conceptual metaphor *religion is a journey* by the journey frame that may involve a lovely garden as a place where the journey leads.

The mention of "Janna جنّة " is very frequent in Qur'an, and it is often related to a rich image describing rivers and food and drink and sensual pleasures that the journeyer may enjoy once arriving to his destination:

> "(..)and surely I shall bring you into <u>Gardens</u> underneath which rivers flow." (Maida5/12).
> "The righteous [will be] in <u>gardens</u> and fountains [of clear- flowing water]." (Al-Hijr15/45).
> "With it We grow for you <u>gardens</u> of date-palms and vines: in them have ye abundant fruits: and of them ye eat [and have enjoyment]." (Muminun23/19).
> "<u>Gardens</u> of Eternity will they enter: there in will they be adorned with bracelets of gold and pearls; and their garments there will be of silk." (Fatir35/33).
> "They will recline [with ease] on <u>Thrones [of dignity]</u> arranged in ranks; and we shall join them to Companions, with beautiful big and lustrous eyes." (Tur52/20).

What this lexical network shows is the expansion of the journey frame in structuring the concept of religion by the concentration of its linguistic realizations through *religion is journey* metaphor in Qur'anic Text. This predominance stemmed from the capacity of Qur'anic language to analyze the journey frame and blow it apart, and hence, to invest all its scenery components that we have seen. And, at the same time, the target domain of religion was more and more developed and dug into, which led to a variation of its subcategories gathering contradictory notions like belief and disbelief, goodness and sin, reward and punishment.

2.2. Connection of Jihad with Qur'anic lexical network: The expansion of Jihad

We previously argued that Jihad was born inside the blend as a result of the metaphorical projection of the frame of journey onto the domain of religion, this primary appearance of Jihad is followed by an expansion of it through a larger lexical network governing the Qur'anic text. In fact, *Religion is a journey* is connected to other three conceptual metaphors which are *Religion is vision*, *Religion is a trade*, and *Religion is up/down*.(Mougou.2014.) The present section will focus on the description of the connection between the terms realizing those conceptual metaphors and Jihad. Thus, multiple facets of the Mujahid will raise up through the blending operation between different mental spaces leading to the construction of Jihad as a scenario or a rich image constituting the core of Qur'an:

-Connection of Jihad to *Religion is vision*:
This connection is the result of the projection of a multiplication of the blending process, as it is illustrated in (2):

In the first blend operation, the role of the seer (C) in the vision space is projected to the Blend1, likewise the role of Mujahid (B) is projected to the Blend 2 from the journey space, the corresponding value (A) "the believer" in the religion space, is projected to Blend 1 and2, the result is the creation of two blended roles (AC){the believer is a seer} and(AB) {the believer is a Mujahid}.

In the second blend operation, both blended roles (AB) and (AC) are projected to the Megablend in which a unique blended role is created (ABC): {the believer =seer=Mujahid}.

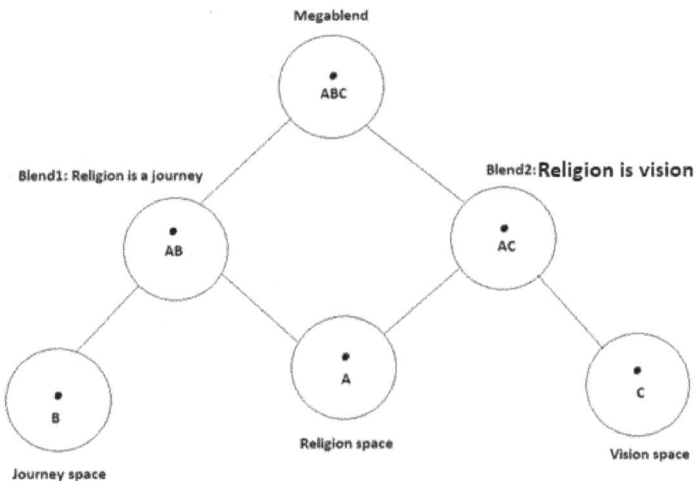

2

Now, we will explore the whole network of blended roles created in the Megablend, this network can be qualified as a part of the theory of Jihad.

– The Mujahid must open his eyes=The believer must know God's truth and apply it.

104. "Now have come to you, from your Lord, proofs [to open your eyes]: if any will see, it will be for [the good of] his own soul" (Anam6/104).

"Our Lord! We have seen and we have heard: Now then send us back [to the world]: we will work righteousness: for we do indeed [now]believe."(Sajda32/12).

"Say: "can the blind be held equal to the seeing?"(Anam6/50).

- In the darkness, the Mujahid is guided by a lamp=The believer must take the Prophet as an example.

O Prophet! Truly We have sent thee as a Witness, a Bearer of Glad Tidings , and Warner. And as one who invites to Allah's [grace] by His leave, and as a lamp spreading light. (Ahzab33/46).

- The Mujahid is guided to the right way by the sunshine= The believer knows the truth through God commandments in its monotheistic religions.

"Allah is the Light of the heavens and the earth. The Parable of His Light is as if there were a Niche and within it a Lamp: the Lamp enclosed in Glass: the glass as it were a brilliant star: Lit from a blessed Tree, an Olive, neither of the east nor of the west, whose oil is well-nigh luminous, though fire scarce touched it: Light upon Light! Allah doth guide whom He will to His Light: Allah doth set forth Parables for men: and Allah doth know all things."(Nur24/35).

"Lo! We did reveal the Torah, wherein is guidance and a light." (Maida5/44).

"And We caused Jesus, son of Mary, to follow in their footsteps, confirming that which was revealed before him in the Torah, and We bestowed on him the Gospel wherein is guidance and a light" (Maida5/46).

"Then those who believe in him, and honor him, and help him, and follow the light which is sent down with him: they are the successful" (Araf7/157).

- The Mujahid is guided by the clarity of the way=The believer has the truth proof in Qur'anic verses and prophets' miracles.

"Thus doth Allah make His Signs clear to you: That ye may be guided." (Al-i-Imran3/103).
"If Allah had so willed, succeeding generations would not have fought among each other, after clear [Signs] had come to them, but they [chose] to wrangle, some believing and others rejecting."(Baqara2/253).

"We gave Moses the Book and followed him up with a succession of messengers; We gave Jesus the son of Mary Clear [Signs] and strengthened him with the holy spirit." (Baqara2/87).

"[Remember also] Qarun, Pharaoh, and Haman: there came to them Moses with Clear Signs, but they behaved with insolence on the earth; yet they could not overreach [Us]." (Ankabut29/39).

– The Mujahid is impeded by the darkness/blindness/death/veil/covering=The believer's faith is ruined by disbelief.
• Darkness.

> Allah is the Protector of those who have faith: from the depths of <u>darkness</u> He will lead them forth into light. (Baqara2/257).

• Blindness.

> "Deaf, dumb, and <u>blind</u>, they will not return [to the path"(Baqara2/18).
> "They have hearts where with they understand not, eyes where with <u>they see not</u>, and ears wherewith they hear not." (Araf7/179).
> "if any will be <u>blind</u>, it will be to his own [harm]: I am not [here] to watch over your doings."(Anam6/104).

• Death.

> Can he who was <u>dead</u>, to whom We gave life, and a light whereby he can walk amongst men, be like him who is in the depths of darkness, from which he can never come out?(Anam.6/122).

• Veil.

> When thou dost recite the Qur'an, We put, between thee and those who believe not in the Hereafter, a <u>veil</u> invisible (Al-Isrã17/45).

• Covering.

We translate here the Arabic word "Kufr كفر" by "covering"(which is not its commonly used translation) because "Kufr"(disbelief) is a term that belongs to the frame of vision since it literally means covering s.th from sight: "Kufr, in its original meaning, is the fact that someone who received a blessing from someone else and denies, it is derived from the root (ك.ف.ر) which means *veiling* and *covering* because the ungrateful person has hidden acknowledging it(..) then, "kufr" became, in Qur'an, a name for polytheism on basis that it is the worst kind of ungratefulness." (Liberation and enlightenment. Vol.1. p.374).

> "Those who covered the Grace of God (who disbelieve) and turn (men) from the way of Allah, He rendereth their actions vain." (Muhammad47/1).

> "Then do remember Me; I will remember you. Be grateful to Me, and <u>cover</u> not Me (ولاتكفرون)." (Baqara2/152).

> "Said one who had knowledge of the Book: "I will bring it to thee within the twinkling of an eye!" Then when [Solomon] saw it placed firmly before him, he said: "This is by the Grace of my Lord!- to test me whether I am grateful or ungrateful! and if any is grateful,

truly his gratitude is [a gain] for his own soul; but if any is <u>covering</u> the truth(وَمَن كَفَرَفَإِنَّ رَبِّي غَنِيٌّ كَرِيمٌ), truly my Lord is Free of all Needs, Supreme in Honor!"(Naml27/40).

– Connection of Jihad to *Religion is a commerce*:

This connection is the result of the projection of a multiplication of the blending process, as it is illustrated in (3):

In the first blend operation, the role of the trader (C) in the trade space is projected to the Blend1, likewise the role of Mujahid(B) is projected to the Blend 2 from the journey space, the corresponding value (A) "the believer" in the religion space, is projected to Blend 1 and2, the result is the creation of two blended roles (AC){the believer is a trader} and(AB) {the believer is a Mujahid}.

In the second blend operation, both blended roles (AB) and (AC) are projected to the Megablend in which a unique blended role is created (ABC): {the believer =trader=Mujahid}.

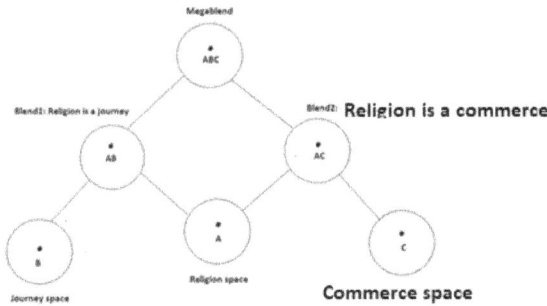

3

– The Mujahid is making a good commerce=The believer chooses Islamic faith.

"O ye who believe! Shall I lead you to a <u>commerce</u> that will save you from agrievous Penalty?" (Saff61/10).

"Those who rehearse the Book of Allah, establish regular Prayer, and spend [in Charity] out of what We have provided for them, secretly and openly, hope for a <u>commerce</u> that will never fail"(Fatir35/29).

– The Mujahid may earn money=The believer chooses to have good deeds or bad ones.

"Every man is a pledge for that which he hath <u>earned</u>" (Tur52/21).

"And if any one <u>earns</u> sin. He <u>earns</u> it against His own soul: for Allah is

full of knowledge and wisdom." (Nisaa4/111).
"Nay, but whosoever hath earned evil and his sin surroundeth him, such are rightful owners of the Fire."(Baqara2/81).
"Unto every man of them (will be paid) that which he hath earned of the sin" (Nur24/11).

- The Mujahid can lose his commerce = The believer can miss his life and his afterlife.

   "Whoso chooseth Satan for a patron instead of Allah is verily a loser and his loss is manifest" (Nisaa4/119).
   "They indeed are losers who deny their meeting with Allah"(Anam6/31).

- The Mujahid buys goods = The believer either exchanges belief with disbelief or the contrary.

The verb (اشترى) in Arabic, is a polysemic verb that denotes both contradictory meaning: to buy and to sell, that's why it is used in Qur'an to mean either belief or disbelief:
It means "belief" in the following verses:

   "And there is the type of man who gives his life to buy the pleasure of
   Allah: And Allah is full of kindness to [His] devotees."(Baqara2/207).
   "Let those fight in the cause of Allah Who sell the life of this world for
   the hereafter."(Nisaa4/74).
   "Allah hath purchased of the believers their persons and their goods; for
   theirs [in return] is the garden [of Paradise]they fight in His cause, and
   slay and are slain: a promise binding on Him **in the Torah, and the
   Gospel, and the Qur'an**: and who is more faithful to his covenant than Allah?" (Tauba9/111).

The same word means "disbelief " in the following verses:

   "These are they who purchase the wrong way at the price of guidance, so their commerce doth not prosper, neither are they guided." (Baqara2/16).
   "Such are those who buy the life of the world at the price of the Hereafter." (Baqara2/86).
   "Those who purchase disbelief at the price of faith, harm Allah not at all, but theirs will be a painful doom" (Al-i-Imran).
   "And believe in what I reveal, confirming the revelation which is with you, and be not the first to reject Faith therein, nor sell My Signs for a small price; and fear Me, and Me alone."(Baqara2/41).

- The Mujahid sells goods = The believer embraces Islam.

   "..then rejoice in the selling which ye have concluded: that is the achievement supreme."
   (Tauba9/111).

- The Mujahid lends money to someone else in order to get it back = The believer gives his soul and his body for God in order to get His satisfaction.

"Who is it that will lend unto Allah a goodly Loan?" (Baqara2/245).
"If ye establish worship and pay the poor- due, and believe in My messengers and support them, and lend unto Allah a kindly loan, surely I shall remit your sins" (Maida5/12).

- The Mujahid is a trader who uses the balance to weigh his merchandise that may be light or heavy, and he must trust the tool he is using = The believer may have good or evil deeds, and he must trust the justice of God in the day of judgment.

"Balance" "الميزان" means in Qur'an human being deeds; the "heavy" balances are good deeds, whereas the "light" balances are bad ones:
"The balance that day will be true [to nicety]: those whose scale will be heavy, will prosper. Those whose scale will be light, will be their souls in perdition, for that they wrongfully treated Our signs." (Araf7/8–9).

"Then those whose balance is heavy,- they will attain salvation. But those whose balance is light, will be those who have lost their souls,in Hell will they abide." (Miminun23/102–103).
"Then shall anyone who has done an atom's weight of good, see it! And anyone who has done an atom's weight of evil, shall see it." (Zilzal99/7–8).

Besides, "Balance" may refer to God's justice in judging people for their deeds:

"And We set a just balance for the Day of Resurrection so that no soul is wronged in aught" (Anbyaa21/47).
"Allah it is Who hath revealed the Scripture with truth, and the Balance." (Shura42/17).
"And the Firmament has He raised high, and He has set up the Balance, in order that ye may not transgress [due] balance. So establish weight with justice and fall not short in the balance." (Rahman55/7)

- The Mujahid is a trader who receives the price of his sold merchandise = The believer may substitute his true faith by material benefits in order to please ignorant people.

"Then woe to those who write the Book with their own hands, and then say: "This is from Allah," to traffic with it for miserable price! –" (Baqara2/79).
"Those who conceal Allah's revelations in the Book, and purchase for them a miserable price, – they swallow into themselves naught but Fire;" (Baqara2/174).
"Nor sell the covenant of Allah for a miserable price" (Nahl16/95).

- The Mujahid is payed for his good work = The believer is rewarded by his Lord.

   "Those who believe [in the Qur'an], and those who follow the Jewish
   [scriptures], and the Christians and the Sabeans, – any who believe in Allah and the Last
   Day, and work righteousness, shall have their pay with their Lord; on them shall be no
   fear, nor shall they grieve." (Baqara2/62).

   "For such the reward is forgiveness from their Lord, and Gardens with rivers flowing
   underneath, – an eternal dwelling: How excellent a pay for those who work [and
   strive]!"(Al-i-Imran3/136).

   "There they will abide forever. Lo! With Allah there is immense pay" (Tauba9/22).

- The Mujahid has an account that will be settled = The believer will be either
  rewarded or punished by his Lord.

   To these will be allotted what they have earned; and Allah is quick in account.(Baqara2/
   202)

- The Mujahid will be fully repaid for what he spent = The believer will be
  equally rewarded by his Lord.

   "But he finds Allah [ever] with him, Allah who repayeth him his due, and Allah is swift
   at reckoning." (Nur24/39).
   "Whatever ye shall spend in the cause of Allah, shall be repaid unto you,
   and ye shall not be treated unjustly." (Anfal8/60).
   "And, of a surety, to all will your Lord pay back of their deeds: for He knoweth well all
   that they do." (Hud11/111).

- The Mujahid is looking for an imperishable commerce = The believer will be
  strongly punished for his bad deeds either during his life or in the afterlife.

   Those who rehearse the Book of Allah, establish regular Prayer, and spend [in Charity]
   out of what We have provided for them, secretly and openly, hope for a commerce that
   will never perish (Fatir35/29).

- Connection of Jihad to *Religion is up/down:*

This connection is the result of a multiplication of the blending process, as it is
illustrated in (4):

In the first blend operation, the role realizing the "up" orientation (C) in
the up/down schema, is projected to the Blend1, likewise the role of Mujahid
(B) is projected to the Blend 2 from the journey space, the corresponding value
(A) "the believer" in the religion space, is projected to Blend 1 and2, the result is
the creation of two blended roles (AC){the believer is up} and(AB) {the believer
is a Mujahid}.

In the second blend operation, both blended roles (AB) and (AC) are projected to the Megablend in which a unique blended role is created (ABC): {the believer =Mujahid=up}.

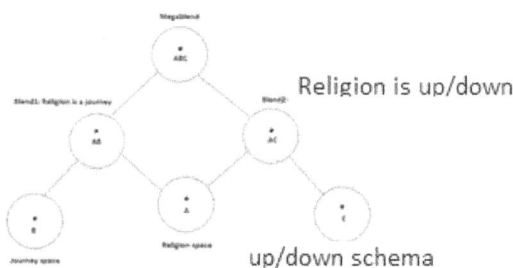

Religion is up/down

up/down schema

4

– The Mujahid is in an upper place, in comparison with the lower place of the non-Mujahid = The believer is honored and venerated, whereas the disbeliever is despised.

"But such as come to Him as Believers who have worked righteous deeds, – for such are the high stations, – " Ta Ha20/75.

"So lose not heart, nor fall into despair: For ye are the upper ones if ye are true in Faith." (Al-i-Imran3/139).
"And he will be in a life of Bliss, in a Garden on high" (Haqqa69/22).
"Day, verily the record of the Righteous is in 'Illiyin. And what will explain to thee what 'Illiyun is? (Tatfif83/18–19).

"Behold! Allah said: "O Jesus! I will take thee and raise thee to Myself and clear thee [of the falsehoods] of those who blaspheme; I will make those who follow thee above those who disbelieve until the Day of Resurrection" (Al-i-Imran3/55).
"then Allah sent down His peace upon him, and strengthened him with forces which ye saw not and made the word of those who disbelieved the nethermost, while Allah's Word it was that became the uppermost." (Tauba9/40).
"And they designed a snare for him, but We made them the undermost" (Safat37/98).

2.3. Religion is balance: Jihad as a component of a schematic projection

Balance is one of the pillars that our physical experience is based on, and in case it is absent, our physical reality would become a big mess. In spite of its importance, we are rarely aware of the existence of balance structure in our life. In fact, balance is a preconceptual body experience, thus it is difficult to be aware of, or to be described propositionally on basis of specific rules. For example, we cannot learn the baby the next step he shall take to be able to walk for the first time, maybe we can try to help or explain or show some examples, but the balance activity itself happens spontaneously without following any rule. We rarely feel balance in our life, unless we lose it through experiences like freezing hands, or very high head temperature, dry lips, which requires doing an effort to get back our balance by warming our hands or wetting our lips and head. Thus, balance seems to constitute a hidden structure or a recurrent pattern that makes our experience significant and coherent, this structure may be manifested through simple events like falling after foot slip and losing one's balance, thus balance becomes noticed because we have lost it, and when we get up, straightness is given back to our bodies. In this example, the fact of getting up would be a kind of calling back for the first distribution of forces, a distribution that is defined according a vertical fictive axis. The same axis can be noticed when we look at a baby trying to walk for the first time, then we notice his first efforts to equally distribute entities and forces while his hands are going up constituting like an horizontal axis in comparison with the vertical one. This fictive axis or central point around which forces are distributed, is not a physical object that we can see, and is not an image that the baby has in mind while trying to walk, and is not a propositional structure or a rule that we consciously conceptualize: it is rather a recurrent pattern in our experience of balance, or what Mark Johnson calls "the schematic image of balance" (Johnson. 1987). Thus, we can define balance schema as the hidden structure that is manifested through a pattern organizing force relations inside our bodily and perceptual experience, this structure can be represented by a fictive point or axis around which forces are distributed either in a balanced or unbalanced distribution.

(5) is an illustration of the prototypical balance schema; it is a schema constituted of a vertical axis on both sides of which there are symmetrical directions that represent a specific distribution of forces around the center.

Besides, there are other forms of balance schema presenting a kind of variations of the prototypical schema: in (6) and (7) the vertical axis is reduced to a unique central point, likewise, force directions distributed around this point, are reduced in two symmetrical directions. The difference between (6) and (7) is that balance in (6) is represented in the form of a twin-pan balance, whereas, balance in (7) has the shape of a point balance. In (8), symmetric forces are subdivided from the same central point, and the internal forces of the circular space are balanced with its external forces.

(5)

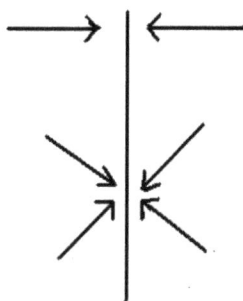

رسم17: محور التّوازن

(6)

(6)

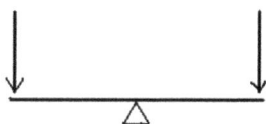

Twin-pan balance

(7)

(7)

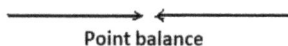

Point balance

(8)

(8)

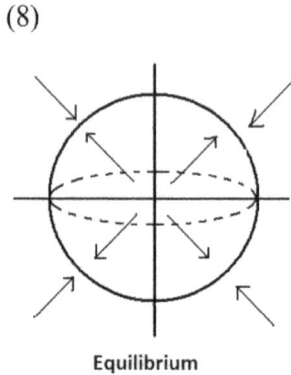

Equilibrium

Balance schema is metaphorically projected onto the domain of religion, there-fore, balance axis and direction distributed around it, are transferred from bodily experience to non-physical domains, and become expressed propositionally. In this part of the book, we will show up the expressions realizing forces that push toward unbalance like in (9), and the expressions realizing forces re-establishing balance like in (10).

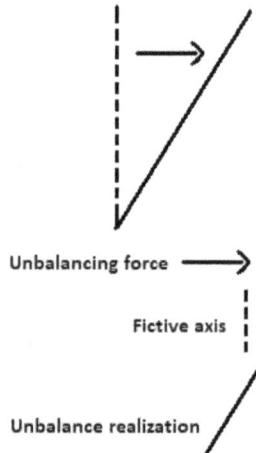

Unbalancing force ——→

Fictive axis ¦

Unbalance realization

(9)

(9) represents the sub-conceptual metaphor *disbelief is unbalance* which is realized in the following expressions that share almost the same original meaning denoting the fact of exceeding the just middle of a way or a place, which is the propositional expression of unbalance schema.

_ To go astray from the straight path:
"Whose among you disbelieve after this will go astray from a straight way" (Maida5/12).
_ To be displaced, to be on the verge:
"Of the Jews there are those who displace words from their [right] places" (Nisaa4/46).
"Can ye [o ye men of Faith] entertain the hope that they will believe in
you?- Seeing that a party of them heard the Word of Allah, and displaced it knowingly
after they understood it." (Baqara2/75).
"There are among men some who serve Allah, as it were, on the verge: if good befalls
them, they are, there with well content; but if a trial comes to them they turn on their
faces" (Hajj22/11).
_ Trial, seduction,temptation.
"Among them is [many] a man who says: "Grant me exemption and draw me not into
trial." Have they not fallen into trial already? and indeed Hell surroundsthe Unbelievers
[on all sides]." (Tauba9/49).

"..but be aware of them lest they seduce thee from some part of that which Allah hath
revealed unto thee" (Maida5/49).
"And their purpose was to tempt thee away from that which We had revealed unto thee,
to substitute in our name something quite different; [in that case], behold! they would
certainly have made thee [their] friend!" (Bani Israil17/73).

_ Profanity :

The most beautiful names belong to Allah: so call on him by them. And leave the
company of those who profane His names: They will be requited what they do. (Araf7/
180).

_ Doing wrong , transgression, to oppress, to be unfair/unjust:

"and the witnesses will say, "These are the ones who lied against their Lord! Behold! the
Curse of Allah is on those who do wrong!-" (Hud11/18).

We said: "O Adam! dwell thou and thy wife in the Garden; and eat of the
bountiful things therein as [where and when] ye will; but approach not this tree,
or ye run into harm and transgression." (Baqara2/35).
_ To commit excesses:

"O People of the Book! Commit no excesses in your religion: Nor say of Allah aught but
the truth." (Nisaa4/171).

"The blame is only against those who <u>oppress</u> men and wrong-doing and insolently transgress beyond bounds through the land, defying right and justice:for such there will be a penalty grievous." (Shura42/42).

_ To belewd/ Wickedness.

"Lo! They were folk of evil, <u>lewd</u>" (The Prophets21/74).

"But Allah has endeared the Faith to you, and has made it beautiful in your hearts, and He has made hateful to you Unbelief, <u>wickedness</u>, and rebellion: such indeed are those who walk in righteousness" (Hujurat49/7).

_ Trespass/rebellion.

"Say: the things that my Lord hath indeed forbidden are: shameful deeds, whether open or secret; sins and <u>trespasses</u> against truth or reason; assigning of partners to Allah" (Araf7/33).
"Allah commands justice, the doing of good, and liberality to kith and kin, and He forbids all shameful deeds, and injustice and <u>rebellion</u>: He instructs you, that ye may receive admonition." (Nahl16/90).

_ Disease.

"In their hearts is a disease; and Allah has increased their <u>disease</u>: And grievous is the penalty they [incur], because they are false [to themselves]." (Baqara2/10).
"And thou seest those in whose heart is a disease race toward them".(Maida5/52).

_ Transgress the limits.

These are the limits ordained by Allah; so do not <u>transgress</u> them if any do transgress the limits ordained by Allah, such persons wrong [Themselves as well as others]. (Baqara2/229).

_ To make by access.

"O Children of Adam! wear your beautiful apparel at every time and place of prayer: eat and drink: But <u>waste not by excess</u>, for Allah loveth not the wasters."(Araf7/31).
"Say: "O my Servants who have <u>made access</u> against their souls! Despair not of the Mercy of Allah: for Allah forgives all sins: for He is Oft- Forgiving, Most Merciful." (Zumar39/53).

_ To overwhelm.(طغيان)

"Go thou to Pharaoh, for he has indeed <u>overwhelmed</u> all bounds."(Taha20/24).
"Therefore stand firm [in the straight Path] as thou art commanded,- thou and those who with thee turn [unto Allah]; and <u>overwhelm</u> not [from the Path]:for He seeth well all that ye do."(Hud11/112).

"In order that ye may not overwhelm [due] balance." Rahman55/8. "the meaning of overwhelming justice is losing it and the weakness of consciousness against injustice" (Liberation and enlightenment. Vol.27. p. 239).

_ Shameful deeds (فحش)

"When they do aught that is shameful, they say: "We found our fathers doing so"; and "Allah commanded us thus": Say: "Nay, Allah never commands what is shameful" (Araf7/28).

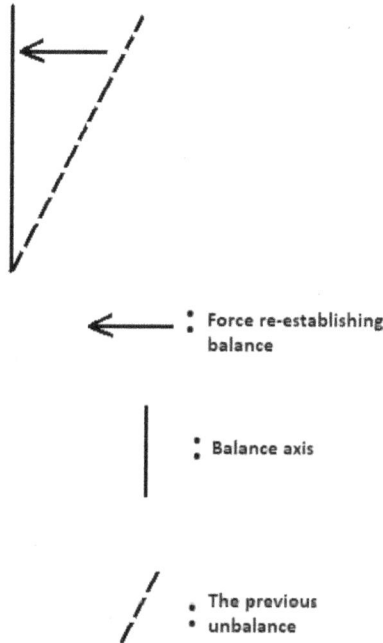

← ⋮ Force re-establishing balance

⋮ Balance axis

/ ⋮ The previous unbalance

(10)

(10) represents the sub- conceptual metaphors *belief is balance* which is realized in the following expressions that share almost the same original meaning denoting the fact of being in a middle of a way or a place, a middle which is a limit that has not to be exceeded, and this original meaning is a propositional expression of balance schema.

_ Guidance to the straight path. (هدى)

Then, when he turned his face towards [the land of] Madyan, he said: "I do hope that my Lord will show me the smooth and straight Path."(Qasas28/22).

"O my father! to me hath come knowledge which hath not reached thee: so follow me: I will guide thee to a way that is even and straight." (Maryam19/43).

"Say: "Verily, my Lord hath guided me to a way that is straight,- a religion of right,- the path [trod] by Abraham the true in Faith, and he [certainly] joined not gods with Allah."(Anam6/161).

_ Righteousness (الرشد)

"Let there be no compulsion in religion: righteousness stands out clear from Error: who-ever rejects evil and believes in Allah hath grasped the most trustworthy hand-hold, that never breaks. And Allah heareth and knoweth all things."(Baqara2/256).

"Amongst us are some that submit their wills [to Allah], and some that swerve from justice. Now those who submit their wills – they have sought out [the path] of right conduct" (Jinn72/14).

"When My servants ask thee concerning Me, I am indeed close [to them]: I listen to the prayer of every suppliant when he calleth on Me: Let them also, with a will, Listen to My call, and believe in Me: That they may be right."(Baqara2/186).

"But Allah has endeared the Faith to you, and has made it beautiful in your hearts, and He has made hateful to you Unbelief, wickedness, and rebellion: such indeed are those who made the right choice;-" (Hujurat49/7).

_ Truth (الحق)

"And say: "Truth has [now] arrived, and Falsehood perished: for Falsehood is [by its nature] bound to perish." (Israa17/81).

"That He might justify Truth and prove Falsehood false, distasteful though it be to those in guilt." (Anfal8/8).

"They say: "Become Jews or Christians if ye would be guided [To salvation]." Say thou: "Nay! [I would rather] the Religion of Abraham the True, and he joined not gods with Allah." (Baqara2/135).

"The true" in this verse, is a translation of the Arabic word (حنيفا) which means "a foot that is inclined" which is rather an unbalanced state of the body. In Qur'an, this original meaning is transformed positively to mean a balanced state of belief, in fact, "hanif" connotes the religion of Ibrahim which was "inclined" from other religions.

_ Justice.

"If ye fear that ye shall not be able to deal justly with the orphans, Marry women of your choice, Two or three or four; but if ye fear that ye shall not be able to deal justly [with them], then only one, or [a captive] that your right hands possess, that will be more suit-able, to prevent you from doing injustice." (Nisaa4/3).

"Ye are never able to be fair and just between women, even if it is your ardent desire" (Nisaa4/129).

"If you judge, judge in equity between them. For Allah loveth those who judge in equity."
(Maida5/42).

_ To requite.

"That Allah may requite each soul according to its deserts; and verily Allah is swift in
calling to account."(Ibrahim14/51).
"Yea, to Allah belongs all that is in the heavens and on earth: so that He
requites those who do evil, according to their deeds, and He requites those who do good,
with what is best." (Najm53/31).

_ Judgment (دِين)

"Dyn" in Arabic, is a polysemic word; it means religion, judgment, account etc. In some
uses of it, it means the requite that people will receive after God's judgment.
"Master of the Day of Judgment." (Fatiha1/4).

_ Law of equality (قِصاص)

"Kisas" in Arabic, means "the compensation of the right of a felony or afine, on a person,
with the same deed, as a measure of justice and halves, hence, "kisas" is used for the
punishment of the culprit by something likewise what he committed" (Liberation and
enlightenment. Vol.1. p. 174.)
"In the Law of Equality there is [saving of] Life to you, o ye men of understanding; that
ye may restrain yourselves." (Baqara2/179).
"We ordained therein for them: "Life for life, eye for eye, nose for nose, ear for ear, tooth
for tooth, and wounds equal for equal." (Maida5/45).

_ To do acts of righteousness.

"but Allah knows the man who means mischief from the man who means good."
(Baqara2/220).
"Whoever works any act of righteousness and has faith,- His endeavour will not be
rejected: We shall record it in his favour" (Anbyaa21/94).
"Help ye one another in righteousness and piety" (Maida5/2).
"As for the Righteous, they will be in bliss" (Infitar82/13).
"Day, verily the record of the Righteous is [preserved] in 'Illiyin." (Tatfif 83/18).

_ To follow a middle course.

"Then We have given the Book for inheritance to such of Our Servants as We have
chosen: but there are among them some who wrong their own souls; some who follow
a middle course; and some who are, by Allah's leave, foremost in good deeds; that is the
highest Grace." (Fatir35/32).
"If only they had stood fast by the Law, the Gospel, and all the revelation that was sent
to them from their Lord, they would have enjoyed happiness from every side. There is
from among them a party on the right course: But many of them follow a course that is
evil." (Maida5/66).

Blending operation in (1) may become more complex (as in (11)) once realizations of *Religion is a journey* are connected to a larger conceptual network that we assume to represent the core of Qur'anic text (Mougou. 2014).

For example, the connection between the following verses prompts for a complex conceptual network illustrated by(2).

"And Allah doth advance in guidance those who seek guidance" Maryam19/76.
"Show us the straight way" Fatiha1/6.
"and follow the light which is sent down with him" Araf 7/157.
"If any turn back after this, they are perverted transgressors."Al-i-Imran3/83

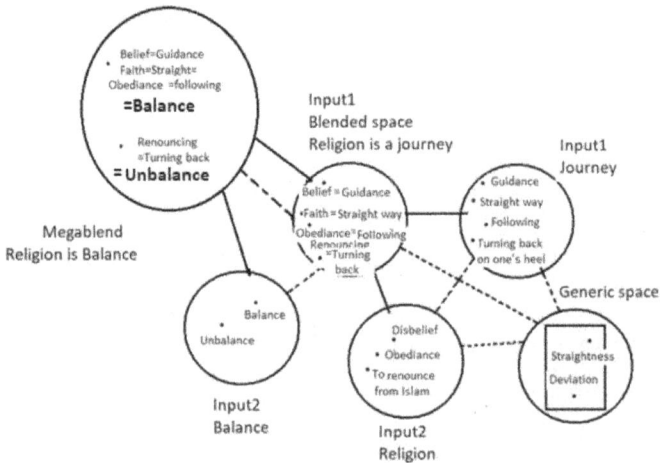

Belief=Guidance
Faith=Straight=
Obediance =following
=Balance

Renouncing
=Turning back
= Unbalance

Megablend
Religion is Balance

Balance
Unbalance

Input2
Balance

Input1
Blended space
Religion is a journey

Belief = Guidance
Faith = Straight way
Obediance= Following
Renouncing
=Turning
back

Disbelief
Obediance
To renounce
from Islam

Input2
Religion

Input1
Journey

Guidance
Straight way
Following
Turning back
on one's heel

Generic space

Straightness
Deviation

(11)

The blending process in the previous verses is based on the following stages:

- The terms {Guidance, straight way, following, turning back on one's heel} prompt for the mental space of the journey.
- The Qur'anic context prompts us to make the correspondence between mental spaces of journey and religion.
- Salience of the values {belief, faith, obedience, renouncing} inside the religion space corresponding to the four mentioned roles.
- both of religion and journey spaces turn into input spaces establishing a selective projection process toward the blended space.

- In the new space, roles are integrated with their corresponding values, as a result, new blended roles are raised: {belief is guidance, faith is a straight way, obedience is following, renouncing from Islam is turning back on one's heel}.
- The connection between those different verses is established through the new roles.
- More compression between roles is needed to clarify the connection between {Guidance, straight way, following, turning back on one's heel}.
- The blended space *Religion is journey* turns into an input space (input1)
- The raise of a new input (input2) representing the balance schema.
- The connection between input1 and input2 is established.
- The activation of a second blending process.
- The creation of the Megablend *Religion is balance* in which more compression happens between the four blended roles.
- The raise of two blended spaces: the first is: {belief/guidance/faith/straightway/following/obedience/=Balance}, the second is: {turning back on one's heel/renouncing from Islam=Unbalance}.

The projection process between spaces, has led to a kind of "fusion" between roles, which generates the creation of the blended space and the Megablend.

The illustration (11) includes the basic constituents of the conceptual integration network: circles are mental spaces, continued lines represent relations between spaces, and discontinuous lines represent connections between inputs and both the generic space and blended spaces. The square represents the structure repeated in all mental spaces called "generic space", this structure is the two schematic elements of "balance" and "unbalance". This schematic structure represents the core of Qur'an and may be translated propositionally in a dual type of Mujahid: Balance=Mujahid who moves in a straight way. Unbalance=Mujahid who moves in a straying way.

The connection between the Generic space and the Megablend is very strong; in fact, they share the same generic space, but this structure seems more specific in the Megablend due to its capacity to include information recruited from the inputs.

The expression "way of Allah" may seem irrelevant since it is based on the combination of two incompatible terms way (concrete)/Allah (abstract). But the expression becomes acceptable and relevant inside the blend. The conceptual metaphor *religion is a journey* is the result of the combination between two different concepts (religion/journey), and this conceptual integration prompts for a linguistic combination realized in "way" and "strive" and a huge number of items spread in Qur'anic text and realizing the same conceptual structure. Some of them will be mentioned later on.

The blend is not a mere addition between different meanings of words, meanings provided by words seem, rather, very little in comparison with meanings that words prompt for. Thus, the blending process between roles belonging to different conceptual domains, seem to be a very creative process.

Chapter 3 Jihad between theory and tradition: Compatibility or opposition

Now that we have enlightened the lexical web of Jihad in Qur'an, it would be difficult to admit that the practice of Jihad in the tradition, is compatible with the philosophy of Jihad in Qur'anic text.

Hence, the internalization of Jihad as a war mirrors a practice found in all cultures and times to varying degrees, the practice of a strong relationship between war and politics both in the East and West. In fact, both politics and war are a struggle for power in order to put certain political, economic, and social ideas into practice. In this process, language plays a crucial role, for every political or military action is prepared, affected, guided, and played by language. To be able to decipher the tight relation between the concept of Jihad in Qur'an as we have analyzed above, and the tradition of Jihad as a political and military practice, we found it necessary to examine discourse of political speaking, namely Barack Obama's Nobel Prize Speech. Given the enormous domestic and global significance of the said speech in times of international economic confusion, it is crucial to look for the main conceptual metaphors laying behind this speech. For this purpose, there are three levels of analysis: *firstly*, presenting the realizations of the main conceptual metaphors found in this discourse, *secondly*, illustrating the conceptual blending network that is at the heart of the simplest possible meaning of this discourse, *thirdly*, proposing a comparative perspective between Jihad's network in Qur'an, and "war" network in political discourse.

1. Presentation of the main conceptual metaphors found in Obama's discourse

The metaphor system in Obama's discourse is based on two target domains: politics and war; both of them represent abstractions and enormously complex situations that need to be understood via a blending process. The three source domains of journey, commerce and balance, are used automatically and unreflectively to understand the complexities and abstractions of the target domains.

Here are the conceptual metaphors resulting from the projection of the source domains onto the target domains, the linguistic realizations of those conceptual metaphors constitute a part of a system devoted to understanding international relations and war, and hence, help us to know more about this system and to have idea of how it functions.

The underlined expressions shown below are widespread linguistic realizations of a metaphorical understanding that structures how we think about war and politics.

1.1. The projection of the journey's frame

Politics is a journey

"for all the cruelty and hardship of our world, we are not mere prisoners of fate."
"Our actions matter, and can bend history in the direction of justice"
"I am at the beginning, and not the end, of my labors on the world stage"
"my accomplishments are slight"
"(..)who have been jailed and beaten in the pursuit of justice"
"The other (war in Afghanistan) is a conflict that America did not seek"
"in an effortto defend ourselves and all nations from further attacks"
"the instruments of war do have a role to play in preserving the peace"
"America — in fact, no nation — can insist that others follow the rules of the road if we refuse to follow them ourselves"
"we all confront difficult questions about how to prevent the slaughter of civilians by their own government, or to stop a civil war whose violence and suffering can engulf an entire region."
"I believe that we must develop alternatives to violence that are tough(able to endure hardship or pain. "Jihad") enough to actually change behavior"
"a lasting peace"
the world stands together as one(the world/America is a journeyer)

Intransigence(refusal to walk in the right way) must be met with increased pressure(balance: "continuous physical force exerted on or against an object by something in contact with it".)

"the effort to prevent the spread of nuclear weapons, and to seek a world without them"
"nations agreed to be bound (walk or run with leaping strides) by a treaty whose bargain is clear."(journey/commerce).
"All will have access(the right or privilege to approach, reach, enter, or make use of something) to peaceful nuclear power"
"those without nuclear weapons will forsake them"
"and those with nuclear weapons will work towards disarmament"
"And the closer we stand together, the less likely we will be faced with the choice between armed intervention and complicity in oppression.
"a tension that suggests a stark choice between the narrow pursuit of interests or an endless campaign to impose our values around the world"
"The suppression of tribal and religious identity can lead to violence"

"these movements of hope and history — they have us on <u>their side</u>"

"At times, it must be coupled with <u>painstaking</u> diplomacy."

"condemnation without discussion — can carry forward only a <u>crippling</u>(causing a person to becaume unable to walk or move properly) status quo(the current state of things)"

No repressive regime can *move down* a *new path* unless it has the choice of an open door.

"and yet it surely helped set China on <u>a path</u> where millions of its citizens have been <u>lifted</u> from poverty and connected to <u>open</u> societies."

"given the <u>dizzying pace</u> of globalization"

For example, the increasingly taking place of political activity at the global level, might be seen as "a dizzying pace", where the very fast competition between states accounted for a very fast pace between steppers or travelers in a long path; this competition carries a justification of war "wars between nations have increasingly <u>given way</u> to wars within nations"

"The non-violence practiced by men like Gandhi and King may not have been practical or possible in every circumstance, but the love that they preached — their fundamental faith in human progress — that must always be <u>the North Star</u> that <u>guides us</u> on our <u>journey</u>"

"I refuse to accept the idea that the 'isness' of man's present condition makes him morally incapable of <u>reaching up</u> for the eternal 'oughtness' that forever confronts him."

War is a journey

"I am the <u>Commander</u>-in-Chief of the military of a nation in the <u>midst</u> of two wars."

"Still, we are <u>at</u> war" (war is a place at which the journeyer is located)

"I'm responsible for the deployment of thousands of young Americans to battle in <u>a distant land</u>"

"a conflict that America <u>did not seek</u>"

"Some will <u>kill</u>, and some will be <u>killed</u>"

"filled with difficult questions about the relationship between war and peace, and our effort <u>to replace</u> one with the other"

"War, in one form or another, appeared with the <u>first</u> man"

"the manner in which tribes and then civilizations <u>sought</u> power and settled their differences".

"philosophers and clerics and statesmen <u>seek</u> to regulate the destructive <u>power</u> of war"

"war is justified only when certain conditions were <u>met</u>"

"if it is <u>waged</u> as a last <u>resort</u> or in self-<u>defense</u>"

"The capacity of human beings to think up <u>new ways</u> to <u>kill</u> one another proved inexhaustible, as did our capacity to exempt from mercy those who look <u>different</u> or pray to a <u>different</u> God"

"<u>Wars</u> between armies <u>gave way towards</u> between nations"

We notice here that the increasingly taking place of political activity at the global level, might be seen as "a dizzying pace" where the very fast competition between states accounted for a very fast pace between steppers or travelers in a long path; this competition carries a justification of war "wars between nations have increasingly <u>given way</u> to wars within nations"

"In the <u>span</u> of 30 years, such carnage would twice <u>engulf</u> this continent" (***War is a monster*** that threatens the journeyer existence)

"America <u>led</u> the world in constructing an architecture to keep the <u>peace</u>"

"The ideals of liberty and self-determination, equality and the rule of law have <u>haltingly advanced</u>"

"We are the <u>heirs</u> (successor/ next in line) of the <u>fortitude</u> (courage/endurance) and <u>foresight</u> (anticipation/provision) of generations past"

"and it is a <u>legacy</u> for which my own country is rightfully proud."

"this old architecture(inherited ideals) <u>is buckling</u> (bend, incline/give way under pressure) under the weight of new threats"

"the prospect of war between two nuclear <u>superpowers</u>"

"<u>Terrorism</u> has long been a <u>tactic</u>"

"wars between nations have increasingly <u>given way</u> to wars within nations"

"In today's wars, many more <u>civilians</u> are <u>killed</u> than <u>soldiers</u>"

"<u>refugees</u> amassed"

"What I do know is that <u>meeting</u> these <u>challenges</u> (problems of war) will require the same <u>vision, hard work</u>, and <u>persistence</u> of those men and women who acted so <u>boldly</u> decades ago"

"a <u>head</u> of state sworn to <u>protect</u> and <u>defend</u> my nation"

"I <u>face</u> the world as it is, and cannot <u>stand(the journeyer stands on his feet "maintain an upright position supported by one's feet")</u> idle (avoiding work in the <u>face</u> of threats to the American people"

"A non-violent movement could not have <u>halted("bring or come to an abrupt stop, a suspension of movement or activity, typically a temporary one")</u> Hitler's armies"

"Negotiations cannot convince al Qaeda's <u>leaders</u> to <u>lay down</u> their arms"

"We have <u>borne</u> this <u>burden</u> not because we <u>seek</u> to impose our will"

"The soldier's courage and sacrifice is full of <u>glory</u>, expressing <u>devotion</u> to country, to cause, to <u>comrades</u> in arms"

"more attainable peace, based not on a sudden revolution in human nature but on a gradual <u>evolution</u> in human institutions"

"What might this <u>evolution</u> look like? What might these practical <u>steps</u> be?"

"The world <u>rallied</u> around America after the 9/11 attacks, and continues to support our <u>efforts</u> (Jihad) in Afghanistan" "the world recognized the need to <u>confront</u> Saddam Hussein when he invaded Kuwait"

"The belief that peace is desirable is rarely enough <u>to achieve</u> it."

"Peace requires responsibility. Peace entails <u>sacrifice</u>"

"Even as we make difficult decisions about <u>going to</u> war, we must also think clearly about how <u>we fight it</u>"

"The Nobel Committee recognized this truth in awarding its first prize for peace to Henry Dunant — the founder of the Red Cross, and a <u>driving</u> force behind the Geneva Conventions."

we have a moral and <u>strategic</u> interest in binding ourselves to certain rules of <u>conduct</u>

"even as we confront a <u>vicious adversary</u> that abides by no rules, I believe the United States of America must remain a standard <u>bearer(carrier)"principles"</u> in the <u>conduct</u> of war"

That is <u>a source</u> of our strength. That is why I prohibited <u>torture</u>

The aim of the journey is to reach "ideals"/God in the religion blend: "And we honor — we honor those <u>ideals</u> by<u>upholding(maintain a practice"</u> them not when it's easy, but when it is <u>hard</u>(Jihad)"

"Those who seek peace cannot <u>stand idly</u> by(idly: with no particular purpose, reason, or foundation. "to see something bad happening without trying to prevent it.") as nations arm themselves for nuclear war."

"a soldier sees he's outgunned, but <u>stands</u> firm to <u>keep</u> the peace"

"she believes that a cruel world still has <u>a place</u> for that child's dreams."

"We can acknowledge that oppression will always be with us, and still <u>strive</u> for justice"

"We can admit the intractability of depravation, and still <u>strive</u> for dignity"

"that is the story of human <u>progress</u>"

War is vision:

"total wars in which the distinction between combatant and civilian became <u>blurred</u>"

We have done so out of <u>enlightened</u> self-interest

"peace is not merely the absence of <u>visible</u> conflict"

1.2. The projection of the commerce's frame

Politics is a commerce

"We <u>lose</u> ourselves when we <u>compromise</u> the very ideals that we fight to defend"

"Those regimes that break the rules must be held <u>accountable</u>. Sanctions must exact a <u>real price</u>"

"For if we <u>lose</u> that faith—if we dismiss it as silly or naïve; if we divorce it from the decisions that we make on issues of war and peace—then we <u>lose</u> what's best about humanity. We <u>lose</u> our sense of possibility. We <u>lose</u> our moral compass".

War is a commerce

"One of these wars (War in Iraq) is <u>winding down</u>."

"And so I come here with an acute sense of the costs of armed conflict"
"It(war) was simply a fact, like drought or disease"
"the seeds of future conflict are sown"
"a consensus that sent a clear message to all about the cost of aggression."
"our actions appear arbitrary and undercut (offer goods or services at a lower price than a competitor) the legitimacy of future interventions, no matter how justified"
"I believe that force can be justified on humanitarian grounds, as it was in the Balkans, or in other places that have been scarred by war"
"Inaction tears at our conscience and can lead to more costly intervention later"
"the role that militaries with a clear mandate can play to keep the peace (keeping money)."
"That's why we must strengthen U.N. and regional peacekeeping"
"…we honor those who return home from peacekeeping and training abroad to Oslo and Rome; to Ottawa and Sydney; to Dhaka and Kigali — we honor them not as makers of war(to make a trade), but of wagers — but as wagers of peace."
"…the question that must weigh on our minds and our hearts as we choose to wage war"
"…our effort to avoid such tragic choices, and speak of three ways that we can build a just and lasting peace."

1.3. The projection of the balance schema

Politics is balance

The projection of the unbalanced axe is realized in the following utterences:

"Those who claim to respect international law cannot avert their eyes when those laws are flouted"
"… cannot ignore the danger of an arms race in the Middle East or East Asia"
"Pent-up grievances fester, and the suppression of tribal and religious identity can lead to violence."

"America's commitment to global security will never waver"
"…in a world in which threats are more diffuse, and missions more complex, America cannot act alone"
"And I'm working with President Medvedev to reduce America and Russia's nuclear stockpiles."
"But it is also incumbent upon all of us to insist that nations like Iran and North Korea do not game(manipulate a situation, typically in a way that is unfair or unscrupulous) the system"

The projection of the balanced axe is realized in the following utterences:

"It (disarmament) is a centerpiece of my foreign policy"
"Those who claim to respect international law"
"America's commitment to global security"
"Those who care for their own security "

"America has never fought a war against a democracy, and <u>our closest friends</u> are governments that protect the rights of their citizens."

"But we must try as best we can <u>to balance</u> isolation and engagement, pressure and incentives, so that human rights and dignity are advanced over time"

"Let us <u>reach for</u> the world that <u>ought to be</u> — that spark of the divine that still <u>stirs(move)</u> within each of our souls."

War is balance

The projection of the unbalanced axe is realized in the following utterences:

"It(war) was simply a fact, like drought or <u>disease</u>"

"…to <u>regulate</u> the <u>destructive power</u> of war"

"…all these things have increasingly trapped civilians in <u>unending chaos</u>"

"economies <u>are wrecked</u>(war is down), civil societies <u>torn asunder</u>"

"<u>Evil</u> does exist in the world"

"To say that <u>force</u> may sometimes be necessary is not a call to <u>cynicism</u> — it is a recognition of <u>history</u>: the imperfections of man and the <u>limits</u> of reason."

"in many countries there is a deep <u>ambivalence</u>(the state of having mixed feelings or contradictory ideas about something or someone. Doubt, uncertainty) about military action today"

"..this is joined by a reflexive <u>suspicion</u> of America, the world's sole military superpower"

"..that brought stability to a post-World <u>War</u> (instability)II world"

"The United States of America has helped <u>underwrite</u>(commerce frame: sign and accept liability under an insurance policy, thus guaranteeing payment in case loss or damage occurs _of a bank or other financial institution_ pledge to buy all the unsold shares in an issue of new securities.)"

"…war promises human <u>tragedy</u>"

"…and war at some level is an expression of human <u>folly</u>"

"But war itself is <u>never glorious</u>, and we must never <u>trumpet</u> it as such."

"…and <u>isolates</u> and <u>weakens</u> those who don't"

"And this (unjustified war) becomes particularly important when the purpose of military action <u>extends beyond</u> self-defense or the defense of one nation against an <u>aggressor</u>"

"This is true in failed states like Somalia, where <u>terrorism</u> and piracy is joined by famine and human suffering"

"it will continue to be true in <u>unstable</u> regions for years to come."

"even as we confront a <u>vicious adversary</u> that <u>abides</u> by <u>no rules</u>"

"those nations that <u>break</u> rules and laws"

"The same principle applies to those who <u>violate</u> international laws by <u>brutalizing</u> their own people"

"For some countries, the <u>failure</u> to uphold human rights is excused by the <u>false</u> suggestion that these are somehow Western principles"

"the way that religion is used to justify the murder of innocents by those who have distorted and defiled the great religion of Islam, and who attacked my country from Afghanistan. These extremists are not the first to kill in the name of God;"
"We make mistakes, and fall victim to the temptations of pride, and power, and sometimes evil".

The projection of the balanced axe is realized in the following utterances:

"The concept of a "just war" emerged"
"..if the force used is proportional"
" ..if, whenever possible, civilians are spared(with no excess) from violence."
"And it will require us to think in new ways about the notions of just war and the imperatives of a just peace."
"And yet this truth must coexist with another — that no matter how justified,"
"will find the use of force not only necessary but morally justified."
"I am living testimony to the moral force of non-violence"
"...America, the world's solemilitary superpower"
"..that brought stability to a post-World War II world"
"...global security for more than six decades with the blood of our citizens and the strength of our arms" open connections between commerce and balance and war."
"The service and sacrifice of our men and women in uniform has promoted peace and prosperity from Germany to Korea"
"...war is sometimes necessary"
"...standards that govern the use of force"
"...adhering to standards, international standards, strengthens those who do, and isolates and weakens those who don't"
"Only a just peace based on the inherent rights and dignity of every individual can truly be lasting."
"...uphold human rights"

"Third, a just peace includes not only civil and political rights — it must encompass economic security and opportunity. For true peace is not just freedom from fear, but freedom from want"

" it's military leaders in my own country and others who understand our common security hangs in the balance."
"no Holy War can ever be a just war"
"for the one rule that lies at the heart of every major religion is that we do unto others as we would have them do unto us."

2. Illustration of the conceptual blending network that is behind Obama's discourse

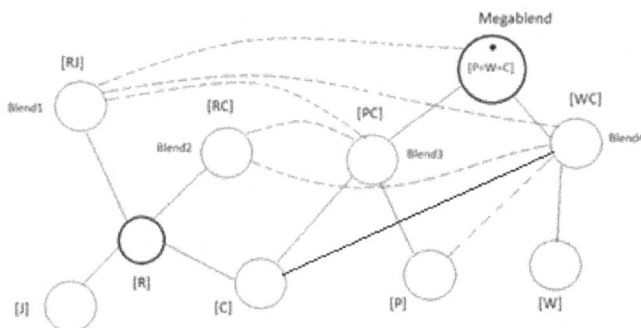

[J]: Journey space.
[R]: Religion space.
[C]: Commerce space.
[P]: Politics space.
[W]: War space.
[RJ]: *Religion is a journey.*
[RC]: *Religion is a commerce.*
[PC]: *Politics is a commerce.*
[WC]: *War is a commerce.*

[P=W–C=balance/unbalance]: possible blended roles between elements from different spaces (journey/war/commerce) and balance image schema.

In (8), it is clear that the religious involvement into politics is based on the common space of commerce, which is a source domain, that is projected onto the target domains of religion, politics, and war.

Literally, there is no semantic relation between the three abstract domains; religion is "the belief in and worship of a superhuman controlling power, especially a personal God or gods", politics is "the activities associated with the governance of a country or area, especially the debate between parties having power", and war is "a state of armed conflict between different countries or different groups within a country".

However, in the conceptual system, as shown in (8), there is an active connection between the three domains, this connection is realized linguistically by lexical items highlighted both in the study of Qur'anic discourse (part1) and in the study of political discourse (part2).

3. A comparison between Jihad's network in Qur'an, and war's network in political discourse

Does political discourse use the same roles that religion discourse uses? Do both discourses share the same roles prompted in commerce frame and projected onto blend 2 and blend 3?

Linguistic realizations that we have seen above show that conceptual structures of the blend 1 and 2, are much richer in blended roles, in comparison with blend 3 and 4, which means that religious exploration of the commerce space is more developed than the political one. In fact, although political and religious discourses use the same source domains (journey, commerce, balance ..), it seems that religious use is much more developed than political one; the tendency in political discourse is to use only terms that connote "conflict" or "extremes". And to explain this, here is a review of the realizations of the conceptual metaphors we have seen in Qur'an, in which shared terms between both discourses will be underlined.

Departure, prepareshimself to a long journey, the first, pace, provision, quits his home, emigration, keeps going along the way leading to his destination,crooked, unrighteous, straight way, straight path, paths, to be devoted to the way he is traversing,Islam,walking waynight, being lost, deviation, right way, to hurry, to flee,following the steps of the right guide, following, guidance, to mislead ,going wrong, turning back on one's heels, turn back, ayat ,to convey (balagh), guardian, protector, arms, power, guardian, brothers, friends of Satan, protectors

to find a refuge(in Allah, from Allah), Burden,charge, the Mujahid, strives, overcome, enemy, war, hardship, Jihad, straight way leading to his destination, arrival, hell, journey's end,destination, slide, deviation, straying, Returning, abode, journey's end, the journeying ,gardens, open your eyes, see,seeing, lamp, spreading light, brilliant, star, luminous, fire, clear, darkness, blindness, blind, veiling, covering, commerce, earns, loss losers buy purchase, price; selling, lend, loan, be heavy, scale, weight, balance, price" pay, account, reckoning, pay back, perish, high, upper high, above nethermost, the uppermost, "undermost", to go astray from the straight path, to be displaced, to be on the verge, trial, seduction, temptation, profanity, doing wrong, transgression, to oppress, to be unfair/unjust, to commit excesses, to be lewed/wickedness, trespass/rebellion, disease, transgress the limits, to make by access, to overwhelm, shameful deeds, guidance to the straight path, righteousness, _truth, justice,_ to requite, judgment, law of _equality,_ to do acts of righteousness, to _follow_ a middle course.

From the survey above, we can have three major remarks:

1 The shared roles between religious and political discourses, are given different values in the blended spaces; for instance: "friends" in political discourse means countries that are supporting America in the war, whereas "friends" in religious discourse refers to people sharing the same faith and protecting each others.
2 Political discourse use many words that are missing in the religious blends, like: terrorism, war.. these words mainly have negative connotations.
3 Many words in the religious blended spaces remained unused in political discourse, like Jihad, pay, light, right path, high.. these words mainly have positive connotations.

Through such lexical relations, the two spheres of politics and religion intermingle, and a few interrogations may be raised: on which ground a political modern discourse, may share the same roles with Qur'anic text? To what extent do the new values assigned to those roles fit into a democratic political system like the American one? In what sense can the conceptual structures shared between religion and politics, stand for a proof that the presence of religion in the political arena doesn't represent a threat to democracy? The discussion above was concerned with these questions.

I think that the combination between language and faith is a very powerful combination. And if political discourse works on more intensive use of positive words in religious text, it will contribute in a large extent, to develop both religious and political thought: the former will be modernized, the latter will be moralized.

We have shown above that religious and political discourses are both a reflection of our imagination, consciousness and thoughts; which involves that both discourses do immensely contribute in creating our reality. In fact, the study of the conceptual metaphors in Qur'an enables us to go beyond the limited-unscientific understanding of religious texts; especially the understanding that suggests there is some force beside of the text receivers that controls the whole world, and that there is a force or God that rewards you or punishes you for what you do.

I want to establish the conceptual structure in the Qur'Bible Text as a science that proves there is no force outside of us and that we are the creators of our world because God is in all of us and He made us in His image. This new science I am calling for proves with scientific arguments that We –as receivers of the religious text- are the operating powers, the world is not operating by itself or by an external force; everything in our reality is created by our way of understanding the religious text, and every word in this text doesn't exist without our imagination and consciousness.

Hence, our lives are affected by our thoughts about Jihad and by the way we imagine it. And if this way is not scientific, then focus will be brought on words that have negative meanings as it was the case for political discourse which had the tendency to vibrate with the negative side of the Balance schema rather than the positive one.

Our values are controlled by the Qur'Bible Text conceptual structures, which do exist in the subconscious level of our collective Mind.

Nothing is true or false in itself. Nothing is good or bad in itself. It's the reader of the text and only him who decides what is bad and what is good, that's why I assume that a new scientific reading to religious texts is necessary and even urgent. Things that the reader assumes to be true in the text, he will believe in them, and they will unintentionally work for him as an autopilot. The science of the conceptual metaphors in the Qur'Bible text will enable us to be conscious of what we imagine and think about main religious concepts like Jihad. And choosing to focus on the positive side of religious thought will certainly lead political discourse and the world toward the greatest destinations. Focusing on positive lexical network that is shared by the Qur'an and the Bible will enable us to develop this Network and expand it in our reality, and this is true based on the universal Law saying that what you focus on expands. When we utter a word, we create the experience of it in our minds, and it will be seen or experienced in the external world either immediately or after a while. By uttering and focusing on the linguistic realizations of the balanced axe in the balance schema, we are choosing a portion of the Quantum field, the portion that is related with the positive energy contained in the balanced axe, and thus, we will be able to create a new positive reality.

Conclusions

In a time that science has explained the world in secular terms and has led to the idea that there is no more need to religion which will fade away, and in a time that technology, social process, cultural mobility, universal education, high lifestyle standards – all were supposed to eat away at religion, in a wash of overlapping acids, a reviving fundamentalism is being spread around the world declaring that religion is going through some kind of "boom". Hence, It seemed careless for politicians to keep misplacing such a large body of people. The connection between fundamentalism and terrorism has led to the shooting of the right parties as an extremist counterpart of the religious extremism. Disconnected from the center of American culture by the intervening secularity of his campaign, Trump's political discourse tends to deal with social and economic and foreign policy problems in purely secular terms. On the contrary, Obama's discourse, as we have seen above, called for a moral revival in America, a return to family values, a strengthening of school discipline, a war on drugs, decreasing of torture, and establishing peaceful foreign policy.

Since the interpretation of religious texts vary dramatically from time to time, and from culture to culture, and purposes and conditions can also vary dramatically, basic mental operations operating over the lexical network of these texts look strikingly important. We need conceptual blending operations because they are products of cognition that vary across cultures although they share the basic cognitive processes.

To conclude, it becomes evident that the interpretation of religious texts should become fuller once neurocognitive theory of meaning is brought in. This book was my attempt to give snapshots of how a scientific religious interpretation might look if we tried to do that. The whole point of a cognitive approach to religion is to aid us in gaining access to the conceptual network that the religious text is based on so that we can, in some extended sense of the term, understand the way we should understand it.

References

Arabic References

القرآن الكريم بالرّسم العثماني وبهامشه تفسير الإمامين الجليلين العلّامةجلال الدّين محمّد بن أحمد المحلّي والعلّامة جلال الدين عبد الرّحمن بن أبي بكر السّيوطي. مذيّلا بكتاب لباب النقول في أسباب النّزول للسّيوطي. قدّم له وراجعه الأستاذ مروان سوار. مدقّق المصاحف لدى وزارة الأوقاف السّوريّة. دار المعرفة. بيروت- لبنان.

ابن عاشور(محمّد الطّاهر):

- تفسير التّحرير والتّنوير. دار سحنون للنّشر والتّوزيع.تونس .
Ibn Achour (Mohammed Taher) : Liberation and enlightenment. Dar Sahnun Edition. Tunisia.

عبد الباقي(محمّد فؤاد):

- المعجم المفهرس لألفاظ القرآن. دار الفكر للطباعة والنشر والتّوزيع.بيروت.

موقو(عفاف): التصوّرات المجازيّةفي القرآن. مقاربةعرفانيّة لبلاغةالنصّ القرآني. جامعة سوسة. كلية الآداب والعلوم الإنسانية بسوسة. 2014.

English References

Abdel Baki (Muhammed Fuad): The Concordance Book of Qur'an. Beirut: Dar El Fikr.

Brown (Gillian) & Yule (George): Discourse Analysis. Cambridge: Cambridge University Press. 1983.

Chomsky (Noam): Aspects of the Theory of Syntax. MIT Press. 1965.

New Horizons in the Study of Language and Mind. Cambridge: Cambridge University Press. First published 2000.

Croft (william) & Cruse (Alan): Cognitive Linguistics. Cambridge: Cambridge University Press. 2004.

Fauconnier (Gilles) & Turner (Mark): The Way We Think. Conceptual Blending and the Mind's Hidden Complexities. First published by Basic Books in 2002.

Fillmore (Charles j.): "Frame semantics", in Linguistic Society of Korea, edited by, pp. 111–137. 1982.

GOD AND MAN IN THE KORAN: Semantics of the Koranic Weltanschauung. First published 1964 by the Keio Institute of Cultural and Linguistic Studies. Minatoku, Japan: Keio University.

Ibáñez (Francisco José Ruiz de Mendoza): The Role of Mappings and Domains in Understanding Metonymy, in Metaphor and Metonymy at the Crossroads A Cognitive Perspective, edited by Antonio Barcelona. Berlin, New York: Mouton de Gruyer. 2003.

Izutsu (Toshihiko): The Structure of the Ethical Terms in the Koran. A Study in Semantics. Vol. II. First published 1959. Tokyo, Japan: Keio Institute of Philological Studies.

Jackendoff (Ray): Semantics and Cognition. Massachusetts, London, England: The MIT Press Cambridge. 1983.

Johnson (Mark): The Body in the Mind. The Bodily Basis of Meaning, Imagination, and Reason. Chicago: The University of Chicago Press. 1987.

Kovecses (Zoltan): Metaphor. A Practical Introduction. Oxford University Press. 2002.

Lakoff (George): Women, Fire, and Dangerous Things. What Categories Reveal about the Mind. Chicago: The University of Chicago Press. 1987.

The Contemporary Theory of Metaphor. market a henson.cc.wwu.edu.@ Copyright George Lakoff. 1992.

The Contemporary Theory of Metaphor, in Ortony (Andrew): Metaphor and Thought, Second Edition, edited by Andrew Ortony. Cambridge: Cambridge University Press. 1993.

Lakoff (George): Philosophy in the Flesh. The Embodied Mind and Its Challenge to Western Thought. New York. 1999.

Lakoff (George) & Johnson (Mark): Metaphors We Live By. Chicago: University of Chicago Press.1980.

Lakoff(George) & Turner (Mark): More than Cool Reason,A Field Guide to Poetic Metaphor. Chicago: The University of Chicago Press. 1989.

Langacker (Ronald): Foundations of Cognitive Grammar, Vol. 1. Stanford: Stanford University Press. 1986.

Lee (David): Cognitive Linguistics An Introduction. Oxford University Press. 2001.

Mougou (Afef): Conceptual Metaphors in Arabo_ Islamic Culture. Seminar for "Study in Japanese Universities" : Science and Technology Supporting the Latest Regional Developments. Hammamet 11, 13 November 2011. Organized by Office of University of Tsukuba in Tunis for Japanese Universities. Cooperated by Alliance for Research on North Africa (ARENA),

University of Tsukuba North African and Mediterranean Centre for Research and Education (CANMRE), University of Tsukuba.

Mougou (Afaf): [Conceptual Metaphors in Qur'ǎn (Muslims Holy Book). A Cognitive Approach to the Qur'ǎnic Text.]. Diss. Manouba U, 2010. Sousse: FLHS UP, 2014. Print.

Rudolph (Peter): Jihad in Mediaeval and Modern Islam. Leiden: Brill. 1977.

Searle (John): Metaphor, in Ortony (Andrew): Metaphor and Thought, Second Edition, edited by Andrew Ortony. Cambridge: Cambridge University Press. 1993.

Sperber (Dan) & Wilson (Deirdre): Relevance. Communication and Cognition. Oxford: Basil Black Well. 1986.

Stern (Josef): Metaphor in Context. Massachusetts Institute of Technology. 2000.

Turner (Mark) & Fauconnier (Gilles): Metaphor, Metonymy, and Binding, in Metaphor and Metonymy at the Crossroads A Cognitive Perspective, edited by Antonio Barcelona. New York: Mouton de Gruyer Berlin. 2003.